Urban Teaching:
The Essentials

Urban Teaching: The Essentials

Lois Weiner

Teachers College, Columbia University
New York and London

To Pooski

Published by Teachers College Press, 1234 Amsterdam Avenue, New York, NY 10027

Library of Congress Cataloging-in-Publication Data

Weiner, Lois.
    Urban teaching : the essentials / Lois Weiner.
      p. cm.
    ISBN 0-8077-3780-1 (paper : alk. paper)
    1. Education, Urban—United States. 2. Teachers—Training of—
United States. 3. Urban schools—United States. 4. Minorities—
Education—United States. 5. Teaching—Social aspects—United
States. I. Title.
    LC5119.8.W45 1999
    371'.009173'2—dc21   98-45410

ISBN 0-8077-3780-1 (paper)

Printed on acid-free paper

Manufactured in the United States of America

06 05 04 03 02 01 00 99   8 7 6 5 4 3 2 1

Contents

Introduction

I've written this book to help new and prospective city teachers become acquainted with both the practical problems they are likely to encounter in their jobs and the moral dimensions of their new occupation. The advice I offer draws on my career as a classroom teacher in suburban and urban schools and on my work as a teacher educator and researcher.

My earlier book, *Preparing Teachers for Urban Schools: Lessons from Thirty Years of School Reform* (Teachers College Press, 1993), synthesizes and analyzes research on urban teacher preparation. This volume is quite different. It is not a scholarly exposition in the traditional sense because I do not attempt to synthesize research and present it objectively to the reader. On the contrary, the book is written in my voice and presents my opinions on several topics that are hotly debated. On the other hand, the book is something other than an extended essay because the opinions I present have been informed by my analysis of a great deal of scholarship about urban schools in particular and curriculum and teaching in general. Readers who are acquainted with research on urban school reform will probably identify here concepts they have read about elsewhere, but I have avoided citations and references to other works for the sake of making the text as readable as possible, as close to a personal conversation as I could make it.

I have two reasons for having used this format. First, I have found that the books that have made the greatest impression on students in my education classes are those that have a clear authorial voice and present life in classrooms as teachers and students experience it. Second, I think that teachers must be critical thinkers, and in this volume I attempt to model the ways in which I hope they will think about their classrooms and educational issues.

When I completed my doctorate in 1990, I worried that I would lose touch with the reality of teaching in urban schools. Though I no longer have a high school classroom of my own, I am in urban schools two or three days a week, working closely with students who are learning how to teach. My graduate classes contain thoughtful teachers who have given me far more information and insight about the texture of life in their schools and districts than I ever could have acquired as a classroom teacher in one school.

My students have been my greatest source of information about teaching, and over the years I have learned as much from friends who are city teachers as I have from books and journals. My colleagues at New Jersey City University, formerly Jersey City State College, have inspired me with their commitment to urban schools and their ideas about how we should fulfill our mission as an institution that prepares urban teachers. My husband, Michael Seitz, assists me in my writing and thinking in ways too small to recall and too great to repay.

As was true of my other book, this volume has been improved by the wise suggestions of Brian Ellerbeck at Teachers College Press. It is dedicated to my daughter, Petra Seitz, known in our household as "Pooski." She has many ideas about how urban schools should change, but we'll save those thoughts for the book she writes.

Lois Weiner
New York City, May 1998

1 A Book of Advice for Prospective and New Urban Teachers

I've written this book for city teachers just starting their careers and students in education classes who want to learn about teaching successfully in urban schools. My suggestions are based on what I've learned in two careers—the first as a public school teacher, the second as a college professor and researcher on urban teacher preparation. I've found that students in my college classes can never get enough information from me about what they should be doing when they have their own classrooms, and if they don't have friends who are successful city teachers they have no way to obtain these "insider" recommendations. Nothing can substitute for actually teaching in an urban school, for experiencing the satisfactions, crises, and dilemmas, but having sound advice about what to expect and how to think about the issues can certainly help.

Sometimes the guidance new and prospective teachers receive from acquaintances who are experienced teachers is sound, but at other times the recommendations are problematic. The advice is well intentioned, and it often helps a newcomer survive, but it also oversimplifies the wonderfully complex job of teaching. One example of this is that my student teachers tell me they are often told, "Don't be friendly with the kids." New teachers who take that advice at face value sometimes avoid common mistakes, but they also miss the chance to think through precisely what kind of relationship they want to have with their students and why they think one stance is better than another.

At its best, teaching in city schools is exhausting, exhilarating, frustrating, and fulfilling. In my experience, city teachers work under the worst conditions and yet they have the greatest responsibility of changing and saving lives. Learning to teach under these circumstances can take several years, and during that time many new teachers leave their jobs because they feel too defeated to continue. I've written this book to help you navigate your first years as a city teacher.

I hope you consider the chapters in this book a series of conversations with a friend of the family who taught in city schools for many years and loved her work. What would you want to learn from this experienced teacher? You'd probably want a frank, thoughtful assessment about the qualities you'll need to be successful and accurate information about what to expect when you have your own classroom.

In a nutshell, that's what I hope you'll learn from this book. But in order to assess the advice I'll give you, you should know more about my background. Why should you take my advice, rather than the suggestions you could get from someone else? How does my advice differ from the material presented in textbooks that introduce prospective teachers to their new occupation?

The students in my college classes often remark to me that they value my suggestions about teaching in urban schools because I am an experienced city teacher. For reasons that I explain in an earlier book, *Preparing Teachers for Urban Schools* (Teachers College Press, 1993), only a tiny percentage of college faculty who prepare teachers ever taught in urban schools. Even when the advice they give prospective teachers is accurate, teacher candidates are often suspicious that it's not rooted in a realistic assessment of what it's possible to do in a real classroom. Let me reassure you that the suggestions and ideas I present to you in this book are ones I've worked out during 15 years of public school teaching, 7 in suburban school systems in California and New York, 8 in New York City.

When I made the decision to teach in New York City, where I had lived after moving from California, I knew I was in for a significant change in my teaching life, and though I was nervous, I felt confident. After all, I had been a highly regarded teacher and I had enjoyed working with the "problem" kids in these schools. I was popular with students of all races and respected by colleagues. I had always enjoyed developing materials and figuring out teaching problems. I knew my subject matter, English, and had conscientiously attended to my professional development by taking many graduate courses in addition to earning a master's degree in teaching English.

What a shock I had my first semester as a city teacher! I was totally unprepared psychologically for what I faced in my first months. By November I was wracked with doubt about remaining. I felt diminished and discouraged, and for the first time since acquiring my own classroom, I questioned my teaching ability. Much of my knowledge of teaching seemed irrelevant, and I had trouble connecting with my students as people. I felt a lack of success and saw myself becoming antagonistic to my students, acting like the teachers I had vowed never to become.

However, by April I had begun to enjoy my students, my teaching, and my colleagues, as I had in the past. The next year I was transferred to another school in Manhattan, this one with an even worse (unde-servedly so) reputation. However, I made the change with little difficulty and soon became a well-liked and respected member of the faculty. Over the next decade I taught in three different schools in Manhattan and thrived as a teacher, more than I ever had in the suburbs.

I forgot about my initial introduction to urban teaching as I became accustomed to my new work environment. Occasionally I noticed that my experiences teaching in suburban schools gave me a different perspective on school practices, but I had no reason or opportunity to think about my introduction to city teaching until I began my doctoral work and examined my career. When I recalled my first months as a city teacher, several questions came to mind. Why did I find urban teaching so traumatic those first months? How did I make the adjustment? What did the existing research explain about my experience? How could this knowledge be used to help people who wanted to teach in urban schools? These questions were the subject of my dissertation and my other book, analyzing research on urban teacher preparation over the past 30 years.

Reflecting on my own first months of city teaching, I realized that the conventional wisdom about what made city teaching so hard—that poor, minority kids were difficult to teach—couldn't explain my situation. I had been a confident teacher of poor, minority students in the suburban schools, so something else had caused my difficulties at Julia Richman High School, my first job in the city schools. When I focused on the nuts and bolts of my first semester, I identified several aspects of school life that had caused me grief. I had been nervous about teaching in a school that was racially segregated, one in which teachers were white and the students minority, but I trusted that this would not be an insurmountable problem for me because I had learned how to work with students from many different backgrounds in my previous experience. In the suburbs, my classroom had been well organized but informal, and I had easily won the trust of my students. In the first months at Julia Richman, I had to figure out dozens of ways to get around regulations, procedures, and policies that kept me from being the kind of teacher I had been before.

As is the case in most schools, urban or suburban, at Julia Richman a new teacher was given the worst program. What makes this practice especially pernicious in city schools is that often teachers aren't hired until school has actually begun, so they have no time to prepare, not even a day. I had five remedial classes, mostly ninth-graders, and no appropriate materials; an assignment to patrol the halls; a homeroom of 40+ ninth-graders; three different classrooms, three floors apart. I was used to doing clerical work, but the volume and rigid specifications of the paperwork at Julia Richman overwhelmed me. Taking attendance was a painstaking task, requiring small cardboard strips called Delaney cards set into slotted folders in addition to a roll book for keeping track of grades and attendance. I wasn't shy about asking questions, like how I could get chalk and paper or how photocopying was done, but finding someone to ask was a monumental challenge. The secretaries in the main office told me to ask my department head, who was nowhere to be found, and my colleagues were never free when I was. The assistant principal in charge of administration could occasionally be found in his office, but he let me know the second week that I was violating the appropriate chain of command by coming to him with questions and problems. In this school, finding out how to do the most basic tasks was a full-time job.

Homeroom, which began the day, was totally exhausting. I couldn't figure out how to treat the students humanely and still do my paperwork. Within a 15-minute period, teachers had to distribute and collect numerous forms, as well as take attendance using two different methods: sorting computer cards for each student and recording attendance in a binder with special symbols. Learning the students' names and matching names with faces was itself a problem, because attendance was very spotty. Many students were repeating ninth grade for the second, third, or fourth time; they visited homeroom and school only on the first of the month to receive their subway passes for free transportation. I had several 17-year-olds registered in my homeroom, and I learned that each term they were issued the same computer-generated program of courses they had failed the previous semester. I was their only contact with the school, and I saw them only for 15 minutes a month!

Other aspects of school life also disoriented me. Like many urban schools, Julia Richman was racially segregated. It had few African American or Spanish-speaking faculty although the students were black, Dominican, and Puerto Rican. Almost all of my own education and teaching had occurred in desegregated settings, and I was used to teaching amid racial tensions, but Julia Richman was a tinderbox. Though never publicly discussed, racial tensions—between Hispanic and black students, between students and white faculty—were physically palpable. Seemingly mundane disagreements immediately assumed racial dimensions. More than once I was called a "white bitch," and I commonly heard students hurl racist epithets at one another. Yet I was left on my own to figure out how I should navigate racial issues with students.

What abilities, knowledge, and attitudes helped me to overcome these barriers to successful teaching? When I analyzed my experience I realized that my preparation to teach had been inadequate, but I had acquired the ability to reflect on my teaching and improve it without assistance. In addition, when I began to blame the students for situations that were frustrating me, I stopped myself, refocusing on the conditions outside the classroom that were causing the problem. I looked for rational explanations for their behavior, and when I couldn't figure out plausible reasons on my own, I asked the students. For instance, I was overwhelmed by taking attendance because students constantly came late, yet the *worst* error a teacher could commit was to send the attendance binder down late after homeroom. The school's average daily attendance, taken during homeroom, determined its funding, and the administration communicated to teachers that the punctual reporting of every revenue-bearing body in the school that day was the teacher's most important responsibility. I felt caught between the demands of my job and the students' failure to do what they were supposed to do. A colleague told me to lock the door a few minutes after the late bell, to exclude latecomers. This forced latecomers to walk down four flights of stairs after homeroom to the attendance office to correct the record; but it also made them late to their next class. Although I didn't feel right about locking the door, I tried it, in desperation. Students responded to this tactic by beating on the door so violently they shook the frame. Their rage showed me that my first impulse had been correct and that the strategy was inhumane, and I quickly dropped it. I should tell you, as a warning to prospective teachers who may think at this point that I should have stayed the course of the "get-tough" strategy, that the door of the colleague who counseled me to lock out latecomers was set afire not long after she told me to imitate her.

As I struggled to devise a routine that permitted me to complete homeroom attendance on time, I asked students why they were late. Some had family obligations, like taking younger siblings to school; others worked until late at night and grabbed a few more minutes sleep in the morning; but most complained that they depended on the subway and that the trains were notoriously unreliable. Subway trains came late, skipped stations, and were so overcrowded as to be unridable. I weighed the options: I couldn't do anything about their fatigue or family tasks, but I knew from my previous jobs that if I cajoled and applied friendly pressure, I could get a significant portion of these students into homeroom on time. On the other hand, the problem with the trains was a new, formidable problem. I couldn't punish students for the Transit Authority's malfeasance, but on the other hand, I felt that I had to help them learn that if the subway couldn't be counted on, they had to leave home earlier. I asked students in homeroom for their suggestions and negotiated a method of taking attendance that satisfied us all: I sorted the computer cards but did not mark the attendance binder until the last 2 minutes of homeroom, allowing latecomers time to be marked present. At the bell heralding the end of homeroom, a student took the attendance binder to the office, and thereafter late students were obliged to go downstairs to change their record.

The alteration in the way I handled attendance seems so small and insignificant, yet it allowed me to use homeroom to get to know my students, to offer advice and encouragement. Homeroom changed from a trial to an opportunity to be with students in an atmosphere relatively free of academic pressure. My successful adjustment to city teaching was a process of figuring out dozens of small changes like this one, which made me more comfortable and relaxed with my students and gave me breathing room to figure out how I could deal with the racial and social tensions in my classroom.

Since I've become a teacher educator who prepares prospective urban teachers, I've had to analyze how I can teach brand-new teachers to take on responsibilities that were difficult for me as a seasoned professional. The information in this book is a distillation of what I have learned from working with my students at Jersey City State College (now New Jersey City University) and the College of Staten Island over the past several years. Their questions, concerns, and insights have helped me to understand more clearly what new urban teachers need to know. In the process of trying to prepare prospective and beginning teachers, I tried to find a book that described how a new teacher could overcome the obstacles I knew of from my personal experience; finding none, I have written this.

The recommendations I make to you about teaching are rooted in my own values, as a teacher and a citizen, just as your decisions about what and how to teach are framed by your beliefs, consciously acknowledged or not. You should, therefore, want to know more about my beliefs about education so that you can weigh the ideas I present against your own. In my role as a researcher and writer, I try to convince educators that we can't understand or change the way students and teachers act in urban schools unless we look at what's different about the urban school setting, rather than examining decontextualized student and teacher characteristics. I discuss this in the next chapter as I explain how teaching in an urban school is different from teaching in other settings. Another idea that influences the recommendations I make is my belief that schooling is a vehicle of limited effectiveness for promoting equality, because many factors that schools and teachers can't control, most importantly the availability of jobs that pay a living wage and quality social services, influence children's development. Although this book is not directly about either of these issues, I think it's important that you understand my perspective on these topics because my point of view influences the advice I give you. As you read this book, you should be thinking about how my values influence the decisions I've made—and how your beliefs will shape your thinking about how to do your job.

My beliefs about education's social purposes and the teacher's role in schooling have also been central to the decisions I've made about how to relate to administrators, teachers, and students. I'm committed to helping all students learn how to think critically and bring their own knowledge and beliefs to bear on making decisions that will shape their lives and our society. I think that the schools should be democratic institutions, in terms of their own practices and organization, and in terms of the values they teach students. As a citizen and teacher, I'm opposed to schools being given the responsibility of ranking and sorting students for the job market.

My ideas about dealing with cultural differences in the classroom similarly reflect my values about cultural diversity in American society. I think that American society has shortchanged itself and minorities by insisting that immigrants, African Americans, and Native Americans deny their cultures and languages to become "real" Americans. The notion that we treat all people fairly when we treat them all the same is a fallacy, especially in education; it denies the histories of oppression and discrimination that influence how students respond to schooling and how schools still regard them. Teachers must be knowledgeable and mindful about the ways in which a child's membership in a social group may influence learning and school success. However, in the last analysis, the key category in teaching and learning is the individual. For this reason, I think that information about cultural differences is best understood as background material that may—or may not—be helpful with a particular student. Poor, minority parents and students can view the disparity between their culture, their language and social customs, and the white, middle class norms of schools quite differently. For some the differences are a barrier to integration into American society; for others they are a strength, to be valued and sustained. I think that teachers should respect the right of parents and students to assimilate or not, as they wish, and to provide students and parents with the information and tools they need to make an informed decision, to give them access to the knowledge and attitudes that the powerful assume and acquire unconsciously. The choice of how to regard power relations in society, however, belongs to students and parents, not their teachers.

The point of view I've explained can be criticized for many reasons. Some researchers and educators may fault my perspective for being individualistic, in terms of both student achievement and teacher performance; other critics may argue that my thinking does not give data about cultural and racial distinctions the primacy they should have in our analyses of teaching and learning. Another argument I've encountered is that I slight the importance of the powerful forces of discrimination and oppression that teachers must counter and explicitly explain. Some educators disagree with my focus on what a teacher can accomplish in her classroom. They contend that the schools are set up to reproduce and justify existing inequalities, so there's virtually nothing the individual teacher can do to reverse this situation.

I think it's possible for good city teachers to hold different opinions about all of these issues about which I've described my point of view. Their decisions about how to approach a particular problem will vary and their classrooms will look different from mine in many ways. However, what distinguishes urban teachers who thrive from teachers who do not is the ability and determination to win, retain, and deserve parents and students' trust. I think that too much energy has been expended on trying to determine the best way to teach, rather than accepting that there are as many ways to organize classrooms and learning as there are talented, caring teachers and specific school contexts. Please don't misconstrue this to mean that "anything goes." Certain teaching strategies are clearly superior to others for communicating information, teaching high-level cognition, or nurturing creativity. But I'm always interested to observe how some people successfully use techniques that I can't, and vice versa. Rather than demanding that all schools and classrooms look the same, we need to try to understand why so many contradictory theories of learning can yield instructional strategies that work well with different children and teachers.

Although you need to learn to adapt to the school setting, you should keep in mind that conditions like mindless regulations and lack of resources are not acts of providence or nature. Unlike the weather, they are the result of political and social decisions that should be changed. Until economic and social conditions outside the school are improved, until urban schools are funded adequately and transformed organizationally, individual teachers will fight a losing battle to reach all of their students. But it is a battle—for children's lives—one in which better-equipped and -educated teachers will do a superior job. I think urban teachers should consider their jobs to be "holding actions" that can't compensate for the effects of racism, for the political and social neglect of cities and poor, minority kids. Yet teachers' efforts to help kids whose only chance of economic mobility is an academic credential affirm the possibility of increased opportunity. I view these efforts as important moral and political acts.

When teaching is the wonderful, intellectually absorbing activity that it can be, most questions that arise are too complex to be answered with formulas. If teaching decisions really take into account the neighborhood, students' personalities and needs, and school culture, no one can give you formulas about how to teach or handle a particular kind of problem. Therefore, this book will not give you recipes to follow—steps to follow in careful order—to produce fine urban teaching. Instead, I try to provide you with frank, accurate information and analysis about urban school systems and advice about approaching situations that are likely to be troublesome.

This book contains no footnotes, endnotes, or bibliography, because I want it to be conversational, and in normal discussions people don't generally give sources to back up their ideas or to let you know the source of an idea. But please don't misconstrue the absence of traditional references to imply that I've written this book without reading a great deal and thinking about it. As I explain in a later section, you will have to take personal responsibility for your own intellectual and professional growth because most urban schools don't provide much help that you'll find useful. As a high school teacher I maintained an active involvement in professional organizations and read as much as I could. Although my recommendations are my own, in the sense that I think they are valuable and on-target, my thinking has been influenced by countless writers and researchers.

The most difficult aspect of writing this book was keeping in mind that I am writing for many different kinds of people who are prospective and beginning teachers. Some of you fit the description of the traditional teacher candidate: a single, monolingual, female from a lower-middle-class or working-class family, raised in a suburb or small town. Others are mature, change-of-career students or women returning to school after sending their children off to school. Some of you are members of groups that have historically not been well served by urban schools: African Americans, Puerto Ricans, Chicanos, Native Americans. Maybe you have emigrated from another country or, though born in this country, identify closely with the culture and language of another nation.

In my own history of teaching and in the experiences of most of the prospective teachers I've taught, I've observed that the key task for a student teacher is developing a clear sense of identity, of who you want to be when you are the teacher, of creating an identity of teacher that is consistent with your personality, values, and beliefs.

In my last year of teaching high school, a student teacher whom I'll call Rebecca Stokes, who was enrolled in the teacher preparation program in a nearby university, took over two of my classes. Rebecca struggled the entire semester over the most basic decisions of how and what to teach; at mid-term she admitted to me that she was still grappling with what it meant for her to be the teacher. She still had great difficulty being called "Miss Stokes" by her students and confided that up until this point in her life the only people who had ever called her "Miss Stokes" were the secretaries in doctors' offices. Who was this mysterious "Miss Stokes" who had the power to call parents, give grades, and pass judgment on students' work?

Who do you want to be as a teacher? For some prospective and beginning teachers, like Rebecca Stokes, being addressed as an adult feels odd. For other new teachers, those who have already experienced many adult responsibilities that require the exercise of authority—like raising children or having a career—acquiring an identity as a teacher is usually less difficult because acquiring an occupational identity is separate from taking on the responsibility of a job. However, more mature students often feel anxious about becoming the "Mr. Brown" who directs a group of first-graders rather than the one who sells books because they are making a significant change in their lives. The stakes feel much higher in this new occupation because the old sense of self has been put at risk. The process of acquiring an identity that fits you is intensely personal. It's a journey that you must take alone.

I hope this book will help you to examine critically your values and ideals about teaching. As I explain in Chapter 4, the greater the cultural and social distance between you and your students, the more essential it is for you to be clear about your own expectations when you assume responsibility for a classroom of students. New and prospective teachers almost always worry more about class control than any other issue, and for good reason. We can't know in advance if we can handle a group of 30 young people in a room together because we've never tried. As I discuss in Chapter 6, your control stems from your moral authority; however, your moral presence depends on your having a clear sense of how you want your students to regard you and how you regard them in your capacity as the classroom leader.

Nothing about urban teaching contradicts the tenets of good practice outside of city schools, but successful urban teaching requires more and better teaching skills and knowledge. I explain in Chapter 2 why the characteristics of urban school systems demand that urban teachers be better at what they do to achieve the same results as their colleagues in suburban schools. If it's harder, why choose to be an urban teacher? Like much in life, it's a greater challenge but the rewards are immeasurably larger, too. The culture in most schools (alas) rules out discussions of teaching's rewards, so there's little chance for teachers to share feelings of accomplishment with colleagues who appreciate how hard-won these victories are. (The last place you'd ever say that you enjoyed your class or did something wonderful would be the teachers lounge!) But the accomplishments can be breathtaking, when we find the opportunity to examine them.

In part because teaching is held in such low regard in our society, I was not particularly proud of being a teacher until I taught in city schools. One spring, I was given an award as "Teacher of the Year" by the local Chamber of Commerce, and I agreed to the honor, provided it was understood that I accepted it as a representative of the dozens of dedicated teachers in my school, Martin Luther King, Jr., High School. In that capacity I attended a ceremony honoring other public employees receiving commendations. The reception was filled with local businesspeople and community activists, and I was at a loss about what to say in my acceptance speech. Right before I was scheduled to receive my award, a firefighter was extolled for an especially daring act of heroism in rescuing an elderly woman trapped in her burning apartment. He had saved a life. What had I done in comparison?

Then I recalled my encounter with Lydia a few weeks earlier. Lydia had been in my ninth-grade English class 3 years earlier. She was older than the other students, and she did no homework, though her reading and writing skills were respectable. Her attendance was irregular, and she was moody; her relations with classmates were often strained. One morning she came into class and started crying. I gave her a bathroom pass so that she could compose herself, and when she returned I found a few minutes to talk with her in the hall while students were working on group projects. She explained that family problems were driving her out of her mother's home and that she was living with her grandmother a great distance from school. I helped her make an appointment with a counselor I knew was empathetic and knowledgeable, suggested some other options, put my arm around her to reassure her, and then returned to the classroom to work with other students.

I didn't see Lydia again for a few years and had forgotten about our exchange . . . so many others like it occurred on a regular basis. One morning she walked into my room, smiling radiantly, to thank me for our talk. She told me I had helped her change her life: She had completed a high school equivalency degree and a job-training program that was paying her enough to save for college. She had enrolled in a community college for the next semester. She was vibrant and hopeful, her eyes luminous with possibility.

Without knowing it, I had rescued Lydia. My act was not dramatic, as the firefighter's had been, and it was not recognized by anyone but Lydia—not even by me until she returned to express her gratitude. But

I had saved a life, and as I told the audience about Lydia, I felt a new, deep respect for the work city teachers do.

Why teach in urban schools? Because you will have the opportunity to help students who need your talent and abilities and dedication. Because you can help save lives while you learn an immeasurable amount about life, yourself, and teaching from your students, who can teach you more than you can imagine.

2 What's Different About Teaching in Urban Schools?

Although I was an experienced, mature, confident teacher who had enjoyed working with students labeled "disadvantaged" in three suburban school districts, my first semester teaching in a typical New York City comprehensive high school was a professional trauma. I felt inadequate and unprepared, and I despaired about my decision to teach in the city schools. However, by the end of the second term I had regained my self-confidence and I spent the next 8 years thriving as a teacher in New York City high schools.

When I looked for answers in research, I found that most scholarship couldn't explain why I had difficulty making the transition, nor why I was successful. Most research took as its starting point the idea that what made urban schools and urban teaching different was the characteristics of students, and much of the research pinpointed the culture of the students and their families as the cause of academic failure. This explanation contradicted my teaching experiences, because my problems in adjusting to city teaching were clearly *not* primarily due to the type of student in city schools. Earlier in my teaching career I had enjoyed working with poor, minority students in suburban high schools but felt overwhelmed teaching the same sort of student in my Manhattan public school.

Distinguishing Characteristics of Urban Schools

After reading 30 years' worth of research on urban teacher preparation, comparing the scholarship to what I had learned in my years of working in urban schools, I decided that by using *inner-city* and *urban* to describe poor, minority students, educators have inadvertently encouraged confusion about what makes urban schools, and the preparation to teach in them, special.

Part of the confusion comes from the fact that cities have always had the greatest concentrations of poor, immigrant students and of children described at different times in the nation's history as "culturally deprived," "disadvantaged," or "at risk." However, the students are only one part of the explanation for what makes urban teaching different. Urban school systems have other traits that create special problems and challenges for teachers. In my second career, as researcher and teacher educator on the college level, I've tried to refine our understanding of what makes urban teacher preparation different. My research and my work with teacher education students have helped me to clarify several factors.

First, there is the matter of the school system's size, its structure, and the role of the school bureaucracy. Urban schools are run by bureaucracies that function quite poorly and are cut off from the communities they are supposed to serve. Since their creation a century ago, urban school systems have been under pressure to resolve political and religious tensions in the nation's social fabric. The school system had to appear to treat all groups fairly, and the method of organization that seemed to do this most effectively was an impersonal bureaucracy. Rules and regulations were put into effect to standardize educational practices and treat students anonymously. However, learning, by its very nature, is an intensely personal, individual matter, so teachers and students in urban schools are caught in a system that undercuts their efforts to allow individuals to learn in the ways that are best for them.

Another important condition that has existed since urban school systems were created is that they have been plagued by inadequate funding. Teachers and students in the nation's cities have consistently faced a scarcity of supplies, materials, and time. For instance, though overcrowding in city schools is in the headlines now, the situation is not new: At the turn of the last century, city classrooms were so crowded that students sat two and three to a desk.

Historically, students in urban schools have been different in terms of ethnicity and religion from students in other areas of the country, and urban school systems have had the responsibility of educating a tremendously diverse group of students. As in the past, today city schools educate a high proportion of students whose families have come to this country to escape political persecution or extreme economic hardship, groups that anthropologist John Ogbu calls "voluntary minorities." But in the past 30 years schools have finally been held to the task of serving communities who share a history of racial discrimination or colonization in this country. These groups, whom Ogbu refers to as "involuntary minorities," were not given equal access to public education until the 1960s, when the civil rights movement called the nation's attention to the injustice of segregation and discrimination. Members of "involuntary minorities" can share memories and personal encounters of persecution and injustice that make them suspicious of schools and school people. Many are apprehensive that adapting to the majority culture will mean losing connections with the community that has sustained them. Schools often respond defensively to parent and student criticism, reinforcing the belief among involuntary minorities that they will not be permitted to use the schools for social mobility, as do the "voluntary minorities."

The characteristics of urban schools that I've identified can be found to a lesser extent in many other school districts. For instance, the largest cities are now surrounded by small, older suburban school systems that resemble city schools in their student population and problems of underfunding. I saw this when I worked in a suburban school district outside New York City, but I also had the opportunity to see that the district's small size meant that communication between district administrators and school-site staff was fairly easy and informal. When I wanted to find out whether a student was correctly placed in my class, I walked down the hall to ask the guidance counselor. If the record seemed inaccurate or incomplete, she'd call across the street to the junior high where the counselor knew the student personally and could correct or confirm the written record. In New York City student records might be kept in three different offices, or they may well have been lost in the student's transition to high school.

In all three suburban school districts I worked in before teaching in New York City, I was the exception in commuting from the city; many teachers lived in the district and the school's neighborhood. I could turn to them for information about the community or a family, to understand my students better. At Julia Richman, some students knew one another from their neighborhood, East Harlem, but almost no teachers lived above 96th Street, the geographical border between Hispanic East Harlem and the white Upper East Side. As a faculty we were socially isolated from our students' lives outside the classroom.

For any school system that receives significant federal or state assistance, as most do today, decisions about curriculum, instruction, and budget are constrained by reams of regulations. But urban school systems have their own separate rules and regulations, on top of the federal and state requirements. The maze of bureaucratic regulation can influence every facet of school life, from your placement in a school to your freedom to open a classroom window more than 9 inches. The larger the school system, the larger and, in most cases, more dysfunctional or "sick" the bureaucracy is.

All over the country school districts are dealing with the results of immigration that have made once-homogeneous school districts culturally and linguistically diverse. However, cities continue to be the first places immigrants settle, so urban schools educate the greatest proportion of new immigrants. Poor children live in rural areas, suburbs, and cities, but the supports that help poor families cope with the problems that accompany extreme poverty are more severely strained by city life. The anonymity of city life further increases the responsibilities schools have for educating children who are hungry, homeless, and subject to violence in their neighborhoods.

I think we can understand what makes urban schools different if we move away from the idea of an either/or answer—*either* a school system is urban *or* it isn't. Another way to define "urban" is to think of "urban-ness" on a continuum, ranging from the largest cities (New York City and Los Angeles) on one pole to the least urban communities (small, wealthy white suburbs) on the other. The extent to which a district can be considered "urban" depends on the configuration and concentration of the factors I've discussed. However, the size of the school system is the key characteristic because the larger the system, the more the bureaucracy intrudes on life in classrooms. Furthermore, teachers, students, and parents have less access to decision making and are more isolated from one another.

Within large urban school systems, conditions in schools vary as much as those in the neighborhoods they serve. In general, schools serving more prosperous, stable neighborhoods have fewer of the characteristics and problems we associate with urban schooling. Although teachers are saddled with the same regulations and policies throughout a school system, the conditions are buffered in schools enrolling students from more prosperous families. Each school in a district receives the same allocation per student for supplies and materials, but teachers who work in schools in middle-class neighborhoods can expect parents to subsidize the supply budget; teachers in high-poverty communities can't. In some respects urban schools that educate students from more middle-class homes are closer on the "urban-ness" continuum to their suburban counterparts than they are to city schools in the poorest neighborhoods, because the schools' capacity to provide intensive support is not as overburdened. When I describe conditions in urban schools, readers should keep in mind that urban schools often differ enormously from one another, depending on their placement on the "urban-ness" continuum.

Prescription for Success: Acquire the Ability to Reflect

How can you be sure that you will not become one of the urban teachers who let the demands of the job overwhelm them? If you didn't start your teaching career with some confidence that you're different from those fatigued, cynical teachers who race the students to the doorway at the end of the day, you'd be ready for retirement before beginning your first job!

But confidence that you're a different type of person is not enough to keep you from succumbing to the roadblocks set in your intended path of helping kids to learn, of making a difference in their lives. The best insurance you can acquire to maintain your idealism and improve your teaching ability is to learn how to reflect on your life as a teacher. The idea of reflective teaching comes from John Dewey, who wrote about reflection in teaching long before I was born. However, his framework in part explains why I was able to make the transition to city teaching, despite my inadequate preparation in education courses: I was able to reflect on my practice and improve it, with no outside assistance.

When I start talking about theory in my education classes, I always see some students respond with a "Not again!" look. I think that as a nation we emphasize the practical and we're suspicious of the value of ideas and theory. That's why we use the phrase "It's academic!" when we describe something as irrelevant or useless. Other societies look to intellectuals and scholars to lead them, but in this country book-learning "is only academic!"

If you have this American tendency to dismiss theory, let me try to convince you that having a framework to analyze how you will make decisions is critical because it helps you to make your professional development *conscious. You* will be in charge of your own growth by having a method of measuring how and what you do in the classroom. Your development won't be hit-or-miss but instead, systematic.

The ability to reflect is valuable for all teachers but it's essential for urban teachers, who are faced with the most morally and politically complex decisions yet have almost no institutional support or help in figuring out how they should behave. In fact, the schools that demand the most difficult moral decision making are generally the ones that provide the least assistance—in any realm. The model of reflective teaching helps you to clarify and articulate how your values influence your decisions about your life in school; it aids you in remaining alert to other perspectives that contradict your own. I'll explain how this works by referring to the crisis in homeroom I described in the previous chapter, to illustrate what each quality involves. However, my brief description of Dewey's ideas should serve only as your introduction to reflective teaching. I strongly recommend that you also read a wonderful book by Kenneth Zeichner and Daniel Liston, *Reflective Teaching* (Erlbaum, 1997). You'll understand Dewey's ideas much more thoroughly if you read the Zeichner and Liston book, which is quite understandable and, frankly, more accessible than Dewey's prose.

Dewey explains that being reflective has three aspects: being wholehearted, open, and responsible. As I struggled to find a solution to homeroom, I demonstrated "wholeheartedness." Other teachers adopted procedures for attendance that angered and alienated the students. A teacher whose classroom was next to mine advised me to simply lock the door at the late bell for homeroom. I tried her solution for a few days, but when the students screamed at me to open the door and beat on the door, I realized I had to look for other solutions. "Wholeheartedness" calls for teachers to seek ways to fulfill their obligations to their students. In other words, "If at first you don't succeed, try, try, try again." The word also connotes an enthusiasm and dedication for your work with children, qualities that contradict the civil service mentality encouraged by the norms and culture of the school bureaucracy.

Students' moral radar quickly identifies teachers who lack wholeheartedness, and such teachers lose credibility and trust. Remember the fate of my colleague who encouraged me to lock the door? An especially angry student set fire to her door.

Dewey uses the term *responsibility* to mean intellectual consistency and responsibility. Although teachers must be conscientious, as the term *responsible* is generally defined, Dewey explains *responsibility* as the ability to critically examine our beliefs and actions in light of the values we profess. In the case of homeroom, I could have solved the problem in other ways—for instance, by staying in homeroom past the late bell to mark attendance and then coming late to the class that followed homeroom. But I value punctuality and believe that teachers should model the habits they want their students to acquire. For this reason, I couldn't be consistent with my values as a teacher and come late to class every day. How could I tell students they had to be in class on time when I arrived late?

Being *open* played a role in my decision because I developed my solution by examining the problem from several perspectives and seeking solutions from many sources. By habit and temperament, I am punctual. I am one of those people who's almost always on time for appointments. My students did not share my regard for punctuality, which frustrated me, but it did not discount the need to understand the situation from their perspective. As I later found to be true almost every time I asked students to explain a problem, their explanation was reasonable.

They pointed out to me that unlike many of their friends, they were coming to school, albeit late. They had difficult commutes on the subway, and many had other responsibilities before school that made them late, like dressing and feeding younger siblings and walking them to school. They felt that their circumstances merited consideration and should be translated into a flexible method for taking attendance. Analyzing the problem from the students' perspective convinced me to swallow my anger at their being late enough to ask them to help me find an acceptable compromise.

In addition to the qualities of openness, wholeheartedness, and responsibility, urban teachers need to understand the way conditions outside classrooms influence the ways teachers and students act. Political, social, and economic circumstances in the school and the community (even the world!), affect our lives as teachers and the decisions we make. Researchers refer to this as the "social context," and if you think about the concept you'll see that thoughtful teachers automatically take it into account. When 15 fire engines and their sirens shriek past your classroom window, the social context of the school is influencing your teaching. Will you try to shout over the noise or pause until the noise subsides? Skillful urban teachers realize that circumstances outside the classroom must be taken into account when they decide how and what to teach. Will you insist that each student bring in a notebook and pencils the first week of school, even when parents, parent, or guardian are unemployed? If you consider factors like this in your decision making, you are making the social context of the classroom part of the process.

Learning to teach in urban schools is not the same as learning to deal with racism in school and society. *All* teachers need to know how to examine their own cultural frame of reference and to understand how social inequality is reflected and reproduced in schooling. Nonetheless, the ability to stand back from ideas and values that we hold strongly—often without knowing it—is most important for urban teachers because the conditions in which they teach *discourage* this way of thinking and operating. Because urban schools are isolated from communities, teachers are cut off from the knowledge parents can provide about their children and their lives outside school. When teachers lack this knowledge and are unable to analyze problems from a variety of perspectives, they frequently blame the students or their families when the kids fail to meet their expectations of behavior and conduct.

In my preparation to teach, no one explained that the social context was an important factor, but my involvement as a political activist—in the civil rights, peace, and women's movements—had made me aware of how outside forces influence our thinking. In addition, I had taught in vastly different settings, so I could see that many of the city's procedures and regulations created problems for students and teachers. My life experiences taught me the importance of the social context before I started to teach, but new teachers can acquire the ability to take factors outside their classroom into account if they develop the ability to reflect.

The idea of reflective teaching has its critics. Some educators argue that teachers don't have the time or energy to reflect because their work lives are totally occupied with other important tasks. Of necessity teachers make decisions mechanically, without conscious reflection, they assert. However, my education students disagree with this analysis of reflective teaching and decision making. They report that they make a semiconscious mental recording of a problem as it occurs in the classroom, and at a later time review the episode they've recorded in their mind. Furthermore, after doing this for a while, they become more proficient and learn how to reflect as a difficult situation occurs.

Reflection does not necessarily produce satisfying solutions. In fact, in urban schools you are likely to encounter a vast number of problems that have no completely acceptable answers. I think urban teachers face more situations that have no satisfactory resolution because their work occurs in a setting fraught with contradiction. Teaching is meaningful for students and instructors only when it is personal and individual; but urban school systems are structured to make schools impersonal and the people in them anonymous. To be successful, teachers must deal with students as individuals, but urban schools were developed to treat everyone interchangeably. The bureaucratic conditions that so heavily influence life in schools make teachers feel like unskilled laborers who are easily replaced; yet the most effective teaching requires an unlimited amount of personal responsibility. Urban teachers must be dedicated to their profession and the people they serve, yet the circumstances of their labor continually remind them that they are hired help.

This contradiction between the demands of teaching and the nature of the workplace make urban teaching very special and very difficult. However, I think that the more clearly you understand how conditions in the school influence your life as a teacher, the better prepared you'll be to make decisions that you can live with and still be a respected, successful urban teacher.

3 Dealing with the Urban School System

In the previous chapter I described what makes urban school systems and teaching in them special. In the next several pages I'll explain how the characteristics of urban school systems influence your life as a teacher and suggest how you can deal with the hurdles created by the system.

The most deleterious effect of the characteristics I've discussed is that they promote your demoralization, making you feel that nothing you can do will help your students. Understanding the sources of your fatigue and frustration won't eliminate them as factors, but if you can accurately analyze the origins of your problems, you'll probably be able to figure out solutions.

Let me draw an important distinction between two concepts that are frequently confused—acknowledging the causes of a problem and excusing it. I think it's correct to say that teachers and students fail to achieve what they could and should in many urban schools, without accepting or rationalizing these failures. In two of the city schools I taught in, many kids did not receive a good education. Almost all the teachers worked very hard and wanted to help their students succeed academically, but the school and school system constantly undermined our efforts. When we managed to step back from the school procedures and regulations to examine them critically, we saw how circumstances outside the control of the students and staff were creating and exacerbating problems in helping all kids achieve their potential. However, teachers in urban schools almost never have a chance to analyze school problems together. As a result, each teacher is on his or her own to figure out how policies and rules are hindering achievement.

Saying that the school system doesn't allow teachers and students to fulfill their potential is very different from saying that children who are not learning what they should cannot learn. In every urban school system you can find some successful schools serving poor children whose families totter on the brink of disaster; in almost every urban school you'll find a few teachers who work successfully with children whom other teachers dismiss as impossible to teach. And you'll find some students that no one has been able to reach.

One of the most stressful aspects of teaching in urban schools is that you will not be able to help each child, although this must be your ideal.

When teachers say that certain kinds of children are uneducable, they are expressing frustration and anger at their inability to teach successfully. Rather than saying "I can't help this kid," they say "This kid can't/won't learn." It's almost never so clear that a child can't learn, and in putting responsibility for academic failure on the student, teachers absolve themselves of any obligation to change their own practices or any of the factors in the school that impede their success in helping children learn what's expected.

When you begin to think that a student or a class is hopeless, you need to summon up the energy to examine the situation critically. One of the first targets for your analysis should be school and district regulations. Almost every policy will have some effect on your classroom, and, more frequently than not, a problem you're having is being caused or exacerbated by some regulation or policy, though its role may not be immediately apparent. Often what you experience is not the foolishness of the regulation but student misbehavior.

Before teaching in New York City schools, I never had significant problems with students' misbehavior, but I found myself battling with my students in my first few years in the New York schools. After a while I saw a pattern in my problems: I was obliged to enforce policies that students (and teachers) disliked, for logical reasons. Many of the regulations made sense in the abstract, but they created tensions between students (or parents) and teachers.

For instance, teachers were supposed to enforce a city policy that called for students to put all outergarments in lockers. Virtually no students followed this regulation, which was apparent when they wore their expensive sheepskin and down jackets to class, no matter what the room's temperature. I nagged, begged, and fulminated, but they continued to wear their coats into the room for the entire class session. On occasion they carried their coats, but they had nowhere to put them because the coats took up a seat of their own and I rarely had empty seats in the class.

The students' behavior seemed entirely perverse to me until I asked an otherwise well-behaved student why she violated the policy. She gave me an "Are you crazy—or what?" look but responded that nobody "wrapped tight"— that is, sensible—would *ever* put *anything* of value in the lockers because they were broken into so easily and frequently. No coat would be secure in a locker, she replied, and her mother had worked too hard for the money that bought the sheepskin for her to let anyone steal it.

As you can see from this situation, the school demanded that teachers enforce a rule that made sense if students had safe places to put their possessions; but under the circumstances, the rule made students choose between obeying a regulation or safeguarding their property. Teachers were responsible for pressuring students to abide by this illogical rule, and if I failed to enforce the rule I risked a reprimand from an administrator who did not see the situation as I did; if I tried to enforce the rule, I confronted my students' wrath and resistance.

In this situation, as in countless others, I had to find a method to skirt a regulation that kept me from treating my students humanely. The strategy I used over the years to figure out an appropriate response consisted of these steps:

1. I examined the problem from the students', parents', and administration's point of view. I assumed that all three parties were doing what they thought best. When I listened to students I frequently saw the problem in an entirely different light.
2. I thought about whose point of view was most consistent with my own values about education. I'd question myself about the purposes of schooling and my moral responsibilities as a teacher.
3. I asked a colleague I respected how she or he handled this particular situation, and why. I'd question the person about the same issues I'd thought about myself: Was this strategy really fair to the students? But I also asked whether the method was practical: Would I be able to defend this method if an administrator questioned its use?

When I followed these steps in the coats-in-class situation, I decided that the rule was intended to encourage an academic milieu. Some parents or administrators might believe that if I didn't enforce the rule I was not teaching students about appropriate behavior in an academic setting. On the other hand, I sympathized with students who did not want to risk having their coats stolen and thought that the administration should first direct its attention to providing secure lockers for students. I decided that students deserved to feel that their possessions were secure in school.

A dedicated teacher who was also the head of the teachers union in the school told me that she had all her students remove their coats and jam them into their seats. When administrators questioned her, she invited them to take over and convince the students to follow the policy. I borrowed her strategy and modified it: I told the students that I understood why they wore their coats and would investigate what the administration was doing to make the lockers secure. When an administrator walked by my room, spotted the bulging coats, and told me that the students would have to take them to their lockers, I explained that they had refused to do this because the lockers were broken into. Rather than generating 10 referrals to the dean, I had brokered this compromise. Satisfied with my answer, the administrator continued his patrol of the corridor.

From my description, the process sounds straightforward, even simplistic. However, several factors make the strategy I've outlined for you quite difficult. One aspect of teaching in city schools that makes analyzing any one issue difficult is that you'll have dozens of problems percolating simultaneously. Finding time and energy to examine any particular issue is a challenge. You have to accept that you're not going to be able to find solutions to every problem at once, so you need to establish your priorities. What's creating the greatest hardship? Tackle that predicament first. In my case, the coats problem had a relatively low priority, so I wasn't able to think it through for 3 years.

A more powerful influence on your behavior is that you and the kids are in the classroom together; the people who make the regulations aren't. So it's natural to focus on what the students should be doing differently and to become angry when they don't perform as you want. The school system's structure and regulations are the hidden offender, but unmasking their culpability takes considerable energy.

What happens frequently is that teachers blame students and parents for not doing what they're supposed to, for not caring about education; parents and students blame teachers for not doing what they're supposed to, for not caring about them. This occurs partly because parents, teachers, and students have no opportunity to collaborate or communicate. Each group feels frustrated, overworked, and unappreciated.

Another factor that makes the three-step process I outlined above difficult to carry out is that we all bring a cultural frame of reference to schools. When our own frame of reference is the same as the school's, we have no reason to question rules that others view quite differently. For instance, if you've been raised in a family that values punctuality, it's hard to understand why some students don't come to class or school on time. Because school norms also support punctuality, it's quite easy to think that caring about education means coming to school on time. Therefore, when kids are consistently late, you may conclude that their families don't care about them or their schooling, especially if the parents are poor and uneducated.

When I share my own experience as a parent with teachers in my college classes, they gasp, shocked to learn that my grade school daughter is 10 or 15 minutes late to school at least once a week. Because my college classes meet at night, my daughter goes to sleep before I come home two nights a week. Obviously I care a great deal about education, but I also value having a block of time with my daughter each day before she goes to school. My priority—having a relaxed breakfast with my daughter when she hasn't seen me for 24 hours—doesn't mean that education is a trivial matter in our family. Yet, if I were not known to be a professor of education, if I had little formal education, teachers would probably assume that my behavior showed a disregard for academic success.

Because urban schools offer so little opportunity for teachers, parents, and students to discuss school practices together, teachers can easily lose sight of alternate perspectives and misconstrue student and parental actions. This dynamic often occurs when teachers have not had life experiences like those of the students and parents they serve. When school people have not endured poverty and racial discrimination themselves, their frustrations make them prey to stereotypes about minority kids. Too often teachers see only the deficits, not the strengths students bring to school. Rather than analyzing what the school and teachers can do differently to help all their students succeed, too many teachers say that "these kids" can't learn because "these families" don't care.

In most urban schools, teachers have more education than the parents of children in their classes, and both parties are aware of this disparity. Because white, middle-class teachers almost never live in the poor neighborhoods from which their students are drawn, the teachers never have relationships with parents in which both parties are equals. Furthermore, if on some occasion in their lives teachers have not had social interaction as equals with adults who are poor and uneducated, they may feel uneasy or even angry when parents who have little formal education themselves make suggestions about their children's education.

Teachers often want to be considered professionals, experts who know what's best for children. This idea of professionalism has value, but it also contains a dangerous element. Although teachers need to have specialized knowledge and skills that parents do not, most parents have a kind of knowledge of their children that teachers seldom can: Parents know who their children are outside school. Yet urban schools do not provide teachers access to parental knowledge and do not give parents access to the teacher's rationale for educational decisions. In most schools, parents only hear from teachers when children need money or a form signed, or when they misbehave. So parent–teacher relations are distorted by an impersonal, bureaucratic setup.

School facilities also discourage the most basic communication between teachers and everyone outside the school. Imagine a business involved in customer service that made 20 employees share a single phone line. Yet that is the situation in urban schools, where classrooms almost never have any means of communicating directly with the outside world. Once you are inside many urban schools, especially those housed in very old buildings, you are incommunicado. When my sister went to the hospital to give birth to her first child, she called me at school and left a message for me to come to the hospital immediately after work. I received the message in my mail slot—2 days later.

How can you deal with this isolation? As you think through problems you face, you need to be mindful of the fact that in your classroom you are cut off from information about your students' lives outside school. As you devise methods of learning about your students and their families, you'll discover their strengths as well as their weaknesses. In most instances, the best starting point in this process is your students themselves.

My advice here is the same I'd give to a teacher anywhere, because good teaching starts with knowledge of your students. The more you know about your students, the more effective you will be because you'll be able to find that lesson or project that will excite them, and you. The more you know about your students as people, the more you'll enjoy your work because *they* will be giving to *you*. When your classroom encourages students to share their ideas, to critically examine the knowledge each person brings to the classroom, diversity becomes an asset. You and your students function like anthropologists learning about unfamiliar neighborhoods and cultures; your students and families educate you and one another.

If you are alert to the necessity of connecting what you do in your classroom to your students' lives outside school, you'll find strategies that work for you in your specific school setting. I think my experience as an adviser of the school newspaper was invaluable in helping me to understand students as people. In the informal setting of a club, teachers and students become acquainted with one another through an activity that requires the teacher's expertise far more than her authority. The understanding and satisfaction you acquire when you work with kids outside of the classroom supports your ability to step back from your frustrations in your role as teacher, so that you can examine classroom problems from other perspectives.

Another method of becoming connected with your students as people is to be active in local community organizations. As a college student in California I helped the farmworkers union organize support for their grape boycott, and I continued this work in my first years of teaching. I didn't realize that it helped me professionally until an irate parent, Mrs. Martinez, came to school to complain about her son Frank's placement in a remedial reading class. Our school contained many students whose parents came from Mexico and spoke Spanish at home, yet we had no programs to help them with the demands of regular English classes, other than placement in remedial reading. My colleagues warned me that Chicano parents could be very hostile about this problem, and they dreaded conferences of this sort. Sure enough, Mrs. Martinez displayed her anger even before our meeting began, waving away my effort to introduce myself. Then she noticed the "Boycott grapes" pin that I habitually wore, and her demeanor changed instantly. She asked if I worked with the union, and we briefly discussed the boycott effort. She and Frank often picketed in front of local supermarkets, and I distributed leaflets at a market near my home. After this exchange, Mrs. Martinez and I were able to work out a less-than-satisfactory solution for Frank, but one that made us allies in trying to change the school's offerings and in helping Frank. Our adversarial relationship changed to an alliance.

If you have not had considerable experience working with city kids, you need to become comfortable being with the kinds of children you'll be teaching before you put yourself in a position of authority. Learning how to exercise authority is almost always difficult for new teachers, and cultural confusion and ignorance exacerbate an already stressful task. In urban schools you simply aren't given opportunities to know your students as people, so you have to bring your own knowledge of their life circumstances to the classroom and on your own become comfortable working with them.

Once you're fairly confident that you'll be relaxed working with city kids, the most efficient method of preparing yourself to face the challenges I've described is to student teach in a school that's similar to the one where you think you'll have your first job. Most of the jobs for new city teachers are in schools that are the most difficult to teach in, and your practice teaching will be most beneficial if you work in a setting that approximates the conditions you'll find yourself in with your first job. Your cooperating teacher will be able to give you many of the practical suggestions for dealing with school policies and rules that you'll be in desperate need of during your first years.

If you attended a segregated school, or an urban school that allowed a high proportion of students to fail, I urge you to student teach in an integrated school that helps all kids to achieve academically. One student teacher I supervised—a remarkably mature, young African American woman who had attended all-black urban schools that failed many students—told me that her eyes were opened when she completed the first phase of her student teaching in a well-regarded suburban school. She was struck by the instructional techniques that could have been used, but weren't, by her own teachers and by the mutually respectful relations betwen teachers and students. If you've already experienced the irrationality of a school bureaucracy and know first-hand how urban schools fail their students, use your student teaching to experience other ways of teaching and learning.

I know that student teaching is a financial hardship on most prospective teachers, and many want to find ways to circumvent the requirement. Because of teacher shortages in urban districts, many systems are now hiring uncertified teachers for schools that are difficult to staff because the neighborhoods are dangerous or the schools are poorly run. You may be able to get a job without having done student teaching, but in most cases your students will pay the price for your lack of training. In some cases new city teachers who have not student taught survive their first years in public school classrooms and go on to have productive teaching careers. In my experience, however, they are the exception. The more difficult the school, the more likely you are to be hired without having done student teaching; however, in these schools the attrition rate for new teachers is generally astronomical.

What about substitute teaching? Isn't that sufficient classroom experience so that you don't need to *pay* the college to work as a teacher? Absolutely not! Working as a substitute gives you practice in controlling a class, not teaching. In important ways it's very poor preparation because it miseducates prospective teachers about the relationship between lesson planning and classroom management. Substitutes must establish themselves as the authority but have no control over the intellectual content or social environment of the classroom. In a teacher's day-to-day relations with students, high-quality instruction is the key to creating a humane, productive classroom.

Almost all the advice I've given in this chapter would also apply to a lesser degree to suburban schools that have many of the characteristics of urban school systems. However, the difference is in the degree. City schools don't allow much margin for error; you and your students pay a high price for your mistakes because the system provides no safety nets. If you handle a confrontation with a teenager poorly, he or she may not return to school for the entire semester, and no one in the school will follow up on the absences; guidance counselors are typically responsible for caseloads of several hundred students. If you don't follow up on a student who's sleeping in your class, no one else will. If you don't notice that a child has a hearing problem, no school nurse will detect it because most urban schools don't have a full-time nurse.

The responsibility is daunting, even overwhelming. In the next chapters I provide you with detailed advice to help you do your job as well as you can.

4 The Urban School Setting

In the previous chapters I've described in general terms what makes teaching in urban schools different from teaching in other settings. For the next several pages I'll discuss how these factors influence your relations with colleagues and your responsibilities as a new teacher. I think this information will help prepare you for the many frustrating situations you'll confront as you begin your career.

Sociologists describe bureaucracies that aren't functioning as they should as "sick." For example, when a bureaucracy is "sick" it can't operate efficiently or fairly; the various units work at cross-purposes; administrators are likely to be either compulsive rule-followers or complete scofflaws. Unless you've tangled before with a "sick" bureaucracy, you probably won't appreciate how much of your work day is influenced by bureaucratic intrusions. Even when your classroom door is closed, regulations and mandates influence your performance, as do illogical, self-defeating procedures you are told to follow. In fact, the foul-ups begin even *before* you've started to teach!

Your First Job

For new teachers the first years are almost always stressful because you have too much to learn. Researchers have found that you're likely to struggle to survive your first year, operating on automatic pilot. By your second year you'll be able to recall ideas you learned in your preparation to teach and apply to them.

The budget for the academic year that begins in September, which often isn't given to principals until after school ends in June, determines the number of teachers a school receives and therefore each person's teaching assignment. Urban schools hire much later than prosperous suburbs, sometimes on the first or second day after the term has begun, sometimes even later. As a new teacher you may be given classes to teach for which you have no formal preparation, because the school needs a teacher for that slot and you're available.

Should you accept a teaching job for which you have no formal preparation? This is an issue of personal conscience, but I'd use as my standard this question: How can you defend accepting the job to the parents of children you will teach? Perhaps you love the subject though you have no formal preparation; maybe you are a quick learner and will seek advice from experienced teachers of this subject; perhaps you've enjoyed working with this age group before and feel that you can master the content because you're so comfortable with the kids. If you can't answer the question with persuasive reasons, you'll probably be utterly miserable for as long as you have this teaching assignment. My advice: *nothing* is worse than teaching in an urban school if you're not having the satisfaction of seeing your students benefit from your presence.

A rational person would expect formal support systems to assist teachers new to the profession or the school, especially in schools that serve students with the greatest needs. This is almost never the case in urban schools. In general, the worse the teaching conditions, the less authentic assistance you'll receive. In most urban schools, new teachers are left to fend for themselves. They are usually observed by administrators because these formal observations are required by law, but the observations are generally pro forma. Rarely does a supervisor have the time to assist new teachers with their eminently reasonable questions and concerns. In the most dysfunctional schools administrators are so overextended that they may never observe new teachers if they trust that they are competent—and perhaps even if they do not. I was not observed my first year of teaching in New York, and a former student teacher of mine who works in an urban school system under state receivership confided that in 2 years of teaching, *no one* had observed him teach. He had received absolutely no feedback, positive or negative, about his teaching from another adult.

This explains a paradox that some wonderful teachers use to their advantage: For their first jobs they are assigned to teach in poorly functioning schools but choose to remain, when they might transfer elsewhere, because they are free from administrative intrusions; they are left alone to teach however they see fit. The other side of this coin is that the same school that houses these fantastic teachers simultaneously allows horrible abuses of many sorts, precisely because there's no oversight.

The struggle for professional survival in these schools is Darwinian: If you can't be entirely self-sufficient in learning how to teach under extremely difficult circumstances, you won't endure with your idealism unimpaired.

Many urban school systems insist that new teachers attend districtwide programs during their first semester or two. The quality and scope of these programs varies widely, but you can probably count on receiving important nuts-and-bolts information about school rules and regulations.

However, most schools offer no comprehensive training or support for new teachers. In response to several national reports about the quality of teaching, many states have mandated mentoring programs for new teachers; but more often than not in urban schools, little mentoring of substance occurs if the program does not contain funding for a reduced teaching load for both the mentor and new teacher, allowing them time to collaborate. If both teach a regular schedule, they have no time to observe one another in the classroom and discuss that observation. Another limitation to these programs is that they frequently do not provide experienced teachers who want to become mentors with appropriate training; so although effective teachers are selected as mentors, they aren't skilled in analyzing or conveying information about what makes them effective.

Unless you're in a highly unusual school, your professional development will be in your own hands. I strongly recommend that if you've had formal preparation to teach, in your first year of teaching you should avoid taking classes in a graduate program. Give yourself at least 1 year to become situated; your work as a teacher will be so overwhelming you won't have the time or energy to spare for college courses. The other advantage to waiting a year or two before you enroll in a graduate program is that your teaching experiences will help you focus on particular areas that need strengthening; another possibility is that after a few years of teaching you'll decide that you want to move into another kind of teaching or school work.

Your Relations with Colleagues

Every school, urban or nonurban, has a different culture, and the culture affects your relations with colleagues. In some schools, especially those with a stable staff, teachers have traditions of sharing resources and celebrating important events. They may have close personal relations with one another—or longstanding feuds. In other schools the staff is totally atomized; holidays pass with only the most perfunctory acknowledgment, and everyone hoards materials.

Despite these differences, urban schools do have certain similarities in their culture that influence your relationships with colleagues. In larger schools relations are more impersonal, and teachers may not even know the names of all the staff, especially if the school is departmentalized. In smaller schools the staff is generally more closely knit. In *all* urban schools, teachers have far more to do than they can accomplish; time is an extraordinarily scarce commodity.

I suggest that from day one you put your radar on, scouting the school for colleagues who can assist you. You probably won't find one person to help you with everything, because no one will have the time. Instead, look for different colleagues to help you with various concerns. You don't need the most dedicated, inventive teacher to tell you how to get chalk, so ask the person whose classroom is next door. On the other hand, if you have a question or concern about how to handle a problem with a student, ask a colleague who seems to enjoy the students, one who talks respectfully to and about them.

I've never taught in a school, urban or suburban, in which staff members freely discussed issues of race and class with one another. Racial tensions are almost always a factor among faculty, but they're almost never addressed. Because our society is so segregated, most of us don't discuss race in integrated settings, and schools don't provide opportunities for teachers—or students—to develop the skills and knowledge needed to examine "hot" issues, like race, with civility.

In another chapter I suggest how you can establish positive relationships with your students, but here I should note that if you are white and your students are not, you will benefit from the perspective that nonwhite teachers can give you about the school and the students. For the same reasons, if your students are not native speakers of English, colleagues who come from the same linguistic and cultural background can often be an invaluable resource. Remember that the school will not provide you with information about your students' lives outside school, so you'll have to find out for yourself who they are as people and how their families and community influence their school work.

For instance, as an English teacher I was struck by the enormous difficulty some of my students who were native speakers of Spanish were having in their writing, in comparison to others who were also Spanish-speakers. I cornered a thoughtful bilingual teacher for possible explanations, and she informed me that Spanish-speaking students in the school came from two groups: Puerto Rican students who had lived in rural areas where compulsory education effectively ended in fifth grade, and South American immigrants, primarily from Colombia and Ecuador, who had lived in cities and were children of relatively well-educated parents. The South American students had learned how to write fairly well in Spanish before coming to this country, so in my class they were able to build on the literacy skills they had developed in Spanish. The students from villages in Puerto Rico were learning how to write while they were learning English. This data helped me reformulate my instruction so that I was more effective with both groups of students, but I might never have understood the differences had I not sought advice from my colleague.

Establishing a professional relationship with a colleague who can be an informant often isn't easy. Bilingual programs are administratively separate in most schools, so you'll have to be proactive to identify teachers who can help you. In addition, the African American teachers who are considered the best by students, parents, and administrators often devote themselves to helping their students directly and aren't active in school life, so you'll have to take the initiative to seek them out. You should seek them out because you can learn a great deal from the way they deal with students, as well as from the way they view the school. As a white teacher, I couldn't be the same with students as the black and Hispanic teachers I respected; but I learned techniques I could adopt.

When I taught in Long Island, I was fortunate to team-teach with a wonderful male African American teacher who was beloved by the students. I could never *be* him, but during our year together I picked up methods of dealing with students that were more effective than the ones I had been using. For instance, he constantly reaffirmed his confidence in them, even when correcting behavior. He would often remind them that their behavior was not consistent with what their mothers had taught them, and he would put misbehavior in personal terms, by telling students who were chatting while a classmate spoke that they were being rude, rather than using the impersonal "Stop talking!" as I did.

Don't be afraid of seeming ignorant or foolish by asking questions, even if your colleagues seem harried and give you short answers. In my experience, though city teachers are very overworked, they remember how difficult their own first years on the job were and want to help newcomers as best they can.

Just as important to your survival as colleagues are nonteaching staff. You should take the time the first few weeks of school to become acquainted with these people who work in the school, especially security guards, secretaries, and janitors. They usually know more about the school's operations than anyone else. However, they're busy, too! Anticipate asking lots of questions, but don't expect a mentor.

In more schools than not—everywhere, not just cities—the discussion in the teachers room tends to be negative; positive comments about teaching seem out of place. Unfortunately, especially for new teachers, it's the last place to go for help in planning lessons because that's not what's done in the lounge. Moreover, schools that have a dissatisfied staff usually have a teachers lounge that exudes demoralization. In general, these are not great places for you to spend your time out of the classroom if you want to retain your idealism. I do know some excellent teachers who spend their free period in the faculty lounge, using the time to chat about their personal lives and refueling psychically. Frankly, I don't understand how they do it. Perhaps you'll be able to filter out the negative, but don't think that you need to bond in the teachers lounge to be respected by your colleagues.

I have tremendous respect for most city teachers, whom I've found to be dedicated and hard-working. However, because the conditions are demoralizing and the school is insulated from parents, even teachers who care about doing their job well may make inappropriate comments about students. Unfortunately, in most schools teachers do not criticize one another publicly for behavior they consider wrong. That's also part of the culture of schools, and not just in cities.

When I heard colleagues insult students in ways I felt were morally wrong and racist, I didn't know how to respond without sounding self-righteous, so I held my tongue but felt that my silence made me complicitous. After a few years I formulated a rejoinder that sounded just right, and I've used it successfully many times. When a frustrated, unhappy social studies teacher said to me "These kids are animals; they need zoo keepers, not teachers," I replied, "Marvin, I know you don't believe that and so you shouldn't say it." Marvin stiffened a minute and then said something like "There was a time I never would have said that, but the fact that I say it shows how burned out I am." On the other occasions when I said "I don't think you really believe that," my colleagues showed momentary surprise but quickly agreed with me that the remark didn't convey how they really felt about their students.

Unless you teach in a very special urban school, you will probably see teaching practices that are indefensible, like teachers who hurl insults at students who misbehave, calling them "stupid" or "animals." I think it's just as important to have compassion for your colleagues as it is to refrain from blaming students or their parents. Remember the distinction I drew earlier between explaining and justifying student behavior that is wrong? This differentiation applies to teachers' performance, too. Although teachers have more power than students—and therefore must assume more responsibility for what occurs in the classroom—they, like their students, are influenced by conditions in the school and the school system. Many teachers are angry and frustrated about the way they are treated by the school system. They feel under attack and unappreciated, insulted by rules and regulations that undermine their self-respect and authority. They sometimes vent their frustration on their students, which is of course totally unacceptable; but in my experience, almost all teachers know when they do this that their behavior is wrong. They need to be (gently) reminded of their better inclinations, reminded about the ideals that inspired them to become teachers.

Often new teachers are angry at what they perceive as malfeasance on the part of more experienced colleagues. I understand the hostility that new teachers can experience toward faculty that they and administrators view as "dead wood." But I have a different way of viewing the situation that may help you to be more understanding about those colleagues you think aren't pulling their load. First, consider how you might regard the school if you had been teaching for 15 or 20 years. The teacher who tells you that you've made a terrible mistake in choosing teaching as a career probably started off his or her career with ideals not too different from your own. Very few people *begin* to teach with a negative attitude, so something happens to them after a while. At the start of your life as a teacher, dwelling on those factors that demoralize your colleagues is counterproductive, but you should recognize them.

Another way of thinking about the demoralization and negativity that teachers project is that there's no way to know for sure how these people act in their classrooms. Because the school structure makes collaboration among faculty very taxing, urban teachers usually see one another in the worst light, as they complain or compete for scarce resources. You don't see first-hand what your colleagues do in their classrooms all day; you only hear descriptions.

Sometimes a teacher who has only the harshest criticisms of her students will devote her time and money to sponsor a club or work with a community group. On more than one occasion I was struck by the inaccuracy of my judgment of a colleague's dedication when I changed my own routine or talked with a faculty member who knew something that I didn't. In more than one instance I learned that a colleague who was a less-than-ideal instructor sponsored an extracurricular activity that regularly kept him at school until nighttime. On other occasions I'd see behavior that didn't fit the conception of the teacher I had developed from negative remarks. Once I left school a few minutes later than usual and saw Mrs. M, a science teacher whom students complained about all the time, leaving the building on a Friday afternoon with two armloads of papers she was taking home to correct. Whenever I saw Mrs. M, she bemoaned our students' abilities and lack of motivation. I had heard students calling her a "bitch" who didn't care whether they learned her subject. She was one of the teachers who'd tell students, "I get paid the same whether you learn this or not." Yet here was Mrs. M overloaded with papers that would occupy her weekend, trying to help her students pass the state exam in science. That's certainly not the way someone who doesn't care acts, but had I not seen her with this work I would never have known how seriously she took her responsibility as a teacher. Many incidents like this have taught me to give my colleagues the benefit of the doubt. They may be disheartened and they may not be innovative or creative, but that doesn't mean that they don't care about their profession or their students.

As I explained earlier, the structure of urban schools cuts off one constituency from another and creates divisions between groups. Few urban schools give faculty common time to plan or discuss shared problems, and teachers frequently have to compete with one another for scarce resources. Young teachers aren't given access to the specialized knowledge older teachers have, and older teachers can't tap the vitality and new ideas their young colleagues bring to the classroom.

If new teachers could see portraits of their cynical, negative, older colleagues when they began their careers, the newcomers would be astonished. Very often teachers who have been working for many years have seen the enthusiasm with which they began their career steadily eroded. When the school system gives them opportunities to replenish themselves, they often do. Unfortunately, urban schools are notorious for the poor quality of their professional development; more often than not, inservice workshops are useless, even insulting. Teachers see that their ideas are not valued or respected, and in response many stop struggling to make themselves heard. They have so often been told to adopt one new curriculum or another that they become skeptical about all change.

Many dedicated teachers respond to the demoralization and alienation within the faculty by focusing entirely on their own classrooms. They shut their classroom doors, literally and figuratively. While this strategy has the undeniable advantage of helping you to ration your energy, the atomization of the faculty makes the school more dysfunctional because many problems can only be solved collectively.

How can you be active in staff life without becoming embattled and isolated? I almost always found that if I acknowledged the extreme hardship of our working lives and followed this with positive suggestions of steps we might take to improve a situation, my colleagues would listen. Like their students, they want to succeed but they feel overwhelmed by conditions that are beyond their control. Your colleagues need your vitality and idealism; you need their knowledge and perspective.

But even as you begin your first years of teaching, you need to think about your future. What will you do to resist the forces that have depleted these teachers? How will you sustain your energy and idealism? Conditions in urban schools will treat you no more kindly than they have your colleagues. You can easily become the teachers whose passivity and negativity make you shudder if you don't think through a personal program for professional growth. You cannot count on the school or your colleagues to nurture your development as a teacher, so join the organizations and professional associations that can keep you intellectually alert and well informed. In the years that I taught in the suburbs, I maintained membership in organizations of English and journalism teachers, and I noticed when I began to teach in the city schools how rarely information that I had taken for granted—for instance, national debates about curriculum—permeated the school walls. It's easy to become isolated in your school, cut off from discussions about developments in teaching and subject areas, so you need to create your own links to the profession.

After you feel that you've become acclimated to your job, talk to teachers who still enjoy their work after many years, and ask them how they've done it. I'm certain they will have helpful suggestions for you. One marvelous social studies teacher I know throws out all her plans after each term so that she starts from scratch each semester; a friend who is a stupendous English teacher creates a new course every few years so that he can teach a current interest; a friend who was a math teacher returned to school for a degree in literature and became a teacher of English in her 15th year of teaching. The strategies are as different as the people, but urban teachers who still enjoy their work after 10 years have quite consciously developed a plan to sustain their satisfaction.

Books, Materials, and Supplies

In most urban schools, materials are a serious problem, especially for new teachers who have not accumulated their personal stash of books, wall decorations, and supplies. Supplies are usually ordered 6 months before you need them, perhaps in April for the following September, and the amount of money allocated is quite paltry. As a result of the chronic underfunding of schools, supplies and teaching materials are sparse, and high-quality materials even scarcer. You should anticipate developing your own.

Most teachers pay for teaching supplies out of their own pockets because they need the materials to do an adequate job. In schools in poor neighborhoods, parents can't provide supplies like pencils, paper, and crayons, so teachers buy them for their classes because they're indispensable. Everyone draws the line at subsidizing the school system at a different spot, and I would never say that one person's limit is morally defensible and another's is not. Teachers face a dilemma: Society and government should fund urban schools adequately, but when kids can't learn because they don't have materials, teachers can't do their jobs well. On principle, I wouldn't buy chalk, though I did purchase pens, markers, and construction paper for journal covers. A friend of mine never bought supplies but provided clothes for needy students. You'll have to decide for yourself how much of your own time and money you're willing to spend because the school doesn't provide you and your students with what you require.

In many schools photocopying is very difficult to do, either because the machines are not accessible to teachers, or because paper is not available, or both. A school with 40 teachers may have only one machine, and you can bet on the fact that it will be broken on the morning you need to run off 25 copies for that day's work. Many urban schools still rely on the rexograph or "ditto" machine for classroom copies, so here again you'll have to decide for yourself whether paying for photocopies, if you can afford it, is a service you'll provide for the school system.

In many urban high schools and junior high schools in poor neighborhoods, teachers are not permitted to issue books until the second or third week of classes. The rationale for this policy is that money for replacing books is scarce, and administrators anticipate that students who are likely to become truant will show up for the first days of the term but not return. If they receive books in these first days, the books will not be recovered, according to this rationale. (Of course if teachers and students are denied texts and do nothing but busywork for the first several days, students will become demoralized, making the rationale for not distributing textbooks a self-fulfilling prophecy.) Be prepared for this predicament. Come to the opening of school with at least one or two weeks of pre-prepared activities that are educationally worthwhile so that students see that your class will be valuable.

The quality of books that you'll find in the school will depend on the specific school and district in which you're teaching, but, in general, the poorer the community the school serves, the worse the resources, including books. Don't be surprised if the school has no books you want to use or not enough books for you to assign one to each student! Many schools give teachers a "classroom set" of textbooks that students can never take home to study or read. The book shortage means that you'll have to create your own materials. This might be a blessing because you won't be forced to use a boring, outdated textbook. On the other hand, you'll be working doubly hard to create these materials rather than supplementing a text.

Space

Most of the time new teachers receive the worst rooms. The physical environment in most urban schools is a disgrace, and the poorer the neighborhood, the worse the maintenance of the school and the classrooms. The only advice I can give you about this is that you have to find alternatives yourself. Let your supervisor know the reasons that the space is creating problems (falling plaster? leaking ceiling? no shades or blinds?), but don't expect him or her to remedy the situation. Repairs can take an entire semester or even a year in urban schools—when they are done at all.

Canvass the school to see what space is available; there may be a room that's free part of the time you need it. Use the space you have creatively, and invest in used furniture if that helps. Here again you'll be personally subsidizing a public school system in the world's richest country, but if a used desk or file cabinet makes your life easier, maybe a handout to the public school system is cheaper than your anguish. If you want to make a change that may be permanent—like putting colored shelf-paper on windows, as several colleagues of mine did to keep the sun from beating down on students—you should mention this to your supervisor.

Clerical Work

Partly because urban schools receive federal and state money earmarked for educating poor children, partly because one unit of the bureaucracy doesn't know what the other offices are doing, urban teachers must complete an unbelievable amount of highly detailed clerical work. The amount of clerical work also depends on the extent to which the state in which you teach regulates curriculum and instruction. Some states, like New York, exert a great deal of control over how and what is taught. Other states, like those in the West, have relatively few regulations, but city and federal regulations combined generate more paperwork than you ever imagined possible. You may have to report attendance for the day, week, month, and term. You'll have to complete forms without knowing their purpose, as well as forms whose purpose is self-evident. All of this paperwork comes on top of grading and lesson planning.

You need a method for handling the paperwork. In my first few years of teaching, I developed a system that helped me deal with student papers and clerical work that kept it from being a sword of Damocles that killed every weekend. The strategy worked well for me when I began teaching in the city schools, though I had to devote more time to paperwork than I ever had before. I always completed clerical work in school, during my lunch hour or "prep" period, and stayed after school a day or two a week to mark student papers and plan my lessons. I know other people who can't face staying at school, so they take clerical work home, to complete while they watch TV, and devote one day of the weekend to planning.

Other people come very early to school. During the first few years on the job, experiment with different techniques to find one that allows you to get your paperwork under control.

If schools were organized and funded appropriately, new teachers would have adequate resources, the easiest teaching programs, and coherent professional support to help them adjust to their new careers. As you can see from my description of the reality you'll encounter, exactly the opposite holds in urban schools. In the next chapter I explain what you can expect from your supervisors and the teachers union as you begin your teaching career in a city school.

5 Your Relations with Teachers, the Union, and Administrators

In most urban schools a kind of warfare exists between teachers and their supervisors. The battle can be a guerrilla operation in which both sides continually snipe or, less frequently, all-out war. In either case, relations are generally strained and hostile. Many new teachers are baffled and demoralized by these enervating battles, so it's important to understand why they occur.

Almost all the points I've made about the difference between teaching in urban and suburban school systems also apply to being an administrator in these settings. In city schools you have to work harder and have better teaching skills to achieve the same degree of success you'd have in an environment that didn't undercut your efforts. The same phenomenon holds for administrators: Only those principals and assistant principals in city schools who are superb administrators can achieve satisfactory results; to really excel they have to be extraordinarily skillful and devote all of their waking hours to the job.

Administrators and Colleagues

As with teachers (and students), the bureaucracy sends school administrators many contradictory messages and provides them with almost no support. In most urban school districts administrators at the school level have remarkably little power to make significant changes in the school's operations. Because decision making is top-down, administrators are put into an occupational double-bind. Being an advocate for the school often means antagonizing higher-ups in the administration, who are responsible for promotions. The system's pressure on the supervisor to enforce foolish rules and policies places the conscientious supervisor in the same quandary as a teacher, but there's a vital distinction: Once teachers are tenured, they do not depend on the supervisor's good opinion of them for career advancement. There's relatively little that a school-site administrator can do to help or harm the career of a tenured teacher; the system's procedures and regulations, including the union contract, limit prerogatives.

Rules and mandates promulgated in the bureaucracy continually threaten successful operations, whether it's an after-school program, a new course, or a new curriculum. One historian who's been involved with many school reform efforts described the bureaucracy's relationship to innovative programs to me this way: Anything different is continually picked at, like a scab, until all distinctive elements are eliminated.

Teachers, who are near the bottom of the hierarchy, depend on the school-site administrators to protect them and their programs. For instance, one year all high schools in New York were mandated to separate ninth-grade students into special units, or "houses," in an attempt to stem the dropout rate, which research showed was greatest in ninth grade. However, Humanities High School, where I taught mixed students of all grades in elective courses, and had a negligible dropout rate. The system's mandate was obviously detrimental to the school's unique curriculum, yet we were subject to it. As the school's spokesperson, the principal had to negotiate the bureaucracy to obtain a waiver. Her ability and willingness to make a case for the school's needs would determine whether it would continue to offer its widely admired elective program. As a new principal, she was in a precarious position; not by nature combative, she hesitated to engage in a battle to protect the school's unusual features. She was able to delay implementation of the initiative, but ultimately the bureaucracy prevailed and the school was forced to comply. Over the course of 5 years all of the school's distinctive features were eroded in a similar pattern, until it became much like any other comprehensive high school.

To obtain their positions, principals must have friends or sponsors within the bureaucracy, and they have to be thought of as "team players." But to protect their schools, they must know how to exert pressure on the bureaucracy; and within their schools they must be perceived as fair and supportive leaders. Unfortunately, people who have this combination of talents, as well as knowledge about sound educational practice and a willingness to work 12 hour days, are rare.

Moreover, someone whose personality and strengths make him or her a fine leader at one school won't necessarily be the best principal of another school, yet urban school bureaucracies deal with school principals and administrators like they do all people, as interchangeable commodities, so they're often plucked from one school, where they've been successful, and placed in another, where they're out of place. Few people naturally have the combination of gifts required to run a school, department, or program, and the school system does nothing to help administrators to develop them. As a result, many people who care about education and children and were respected teachers plunge in over their heads when they become administrators.

One of the department heads I worked under in the city schools illustrates the phenomenon I've just explained. Mr. X, who was chairperson of the English department, was so disorganized and overwhelmed by paperwork that his office, which contained the phones, was entirely covered from the floor to mid-waist in old memos, exams, test papers, and compositions. The phones were buried in these papers, as was his desk, so that teachers would hear the phone ringing but couldn't answer it—because we couldn't find it! Just as importantly, no one could call the security desk or the dean's office in an emergency.

Mr. X was a humane, literate individual who had been a creative, well-regarded English teacher in another high school some years before, but he was not an effective department head for this school. In another setting Mr. X's disorganization would have been less detrimental because the demands made on him would have been more limited. However, Mr. X's weaknesses as an administrator were compounded exponentially by the extraordinary demands made on supervisors in this large, barely functioning comprehensive high school serving students with very poor skills. In addition to overseeing the state exams given in all New York high schools, Mr. X was required to monitor paperwork on countless other projects. Almost all our students qualified for compensatory education courses, a situation entailing substantial recordkeeping: pre-tests, post-tests, purchase orders, and budget reports. Almost all our students took the state competency test in writing two or three times before they passed it. The test was taken in triplicate, but only one copy was sent to the state; the results as well as the actual tests had to be stored in the school.

During my 5 years in the school, teachers in the department were involved in at least 10 different curriculum projects sponsored by the city's division of high schools, the borough office, and a separate curriculum unit; each project, which the department head was obligated to supervise, generated several reams of reports. As the supervisor of dozens of teachers, Mr. X was obligated to write observations of each at least once a year, as well as reports on dozens of ongoing projects. Unfortunately, Mr. X's control of the paper flow was, to say the least, inadequate for the volume of paper the English department generated.

In addition, the school system defined his job as a "line" position, conveying and enforcing regulations, whereas the teachers' expectations were that he would represent their concerns and needs to the principal and the district. Had Mr. X been able to balance these contradictory demands, he would have had some credibility with the staff. However, his gentleness and timidity coupled with his disorganization made him an object of scorn among the people he had to supervise. Accomplishing the most straightforward task, like organizing and grading state exams, became Herculean because relations between Mr. X and department members were so unpleasant.

I've described this situation in considerable detail to demonstrate that the hostility between teachers and administrators needs to be understood in light of conditions in the school system, not just characteristics of individuals. I was no less frustrated than my colleagues with Mr. X's ineffectiveness, but understanding how the demands of the job magnified his weaknesses helped me to maintain a civil relationship.

Still, the strife between administrators and teachers makes life especially difficult for new teachers because if they identify themselves too closely with supervisors who are widely disliked, they isolate themselves from their colleagues. Conversely, if new teachers ally themselves with faculty members, they risk being alienated from their supervisors, who evaluate their performance. You need to keep in mind that your colleagues will not expect a new teacher, one who is not tenured, to become embroiled in conflicts between the administration and the staff. As an untenured teacher you have little legal protection, so you are very vulnerable; and your colleagues know this, even if they don't articulate it to you. They don't expect new teachers to risk their careers by being forthright with supervisors, and you shouldn't have that expectation either.

What if the situation is the opposite—you think the teachers are responsible for the poor relations between administrators and staff? In fact, this was my reaction at the first department meeting: I was stunned at the way people spoke to Mr. X! I had worked with him on a curriculum project the month before school opened and thought him intelligent and sensitive, so I was unnerved by the antipathy that greeted him. As the months went on I saw the department's situation in a different light, and by Thanksgiving I fully appreciated my colleagues' anger.

I think that your point of view about who's culpable may change after you've spent some time as a teacher, so even if you feel quite certain that the faculty is causing problems, bite your lip until you're really settled into the school. Your colleagues will have a very long memory of your actions if you publicly side with a supervisor against them. In my experience these conflicts are seldom so clear-cut that you want to risk your credibility with your colleagues to defend the actions of a supervisor, or vice versa, in your first year or two of teaching.

My advice to maintain cordial relations with colleagues is based on another reality of life in most urban schools. If your situation is typical, your contact with your supervisor will be perfunctory. He or she will probably be too busy to help you out with your classroom, and so you'll have to rely on colleagues for assistance. Another reality is that administrators are under great pressure to attend to superficial details that make the school seem to operate efficiently. The school bureaucracy's greatest concern is the appearance of sound educational practice, not the reality. If you're using a brilliant teaching strategy, no one will see or ask, so your effort won't be acknowledged. Similarly, if no one sees that you're utterly confounded about how to teach a subject, your problem doesn't count as a serious one because it's hidden, so you'll receive neither blame nor assistance. However, if you knowingly or unknowingly violate a regulation and the violation is noticed, the issue will receive immediate attention. Because your adhesion to school rules will receive more attention from most school administrators than your teaching ability, you need to rely on your colleagues for help in your classroom.

What if the negativity of the teachers is so overwhelming, their overt statements of prejudice so frequent that you find yourself totally isolated from your colleagues? If the principal or department head seems sympathetic, you may be tempted to develop a close relationship with the administrator as a way to set the other teachers straight. Trying to take on your colleagues alone, as a new teacher, is quite unwise, even if you seem to have an administrator's support. The comparison may seem grisly, but it's apt: Think of prisoners and the warden. The warden can't protect prisoners' from the wrath of other inmates, and, in fact, doesn't usually make more than a nominal effort because protection of a highly unpopular inmate who's viewed as being a favorite might disrupt the status quo to the point that rebellion would break out.

I have never worked in a school in which my own political beliefs were shared by a majority of the teachers, but for the reasons I've explained elsewhere, I was able to establish a respectful working relationship with my colleagues. However, I realize that my situation is not necessarily shared by minority teachers in schools with a predominantly white faculty, because they may experience more acute social isolation than white teachers who have similar values and beliefs about schooling or politics. The advice I have in this case comes from my colleague at New Jersey City University, who weathered isolation and intense, overt hostility from other teachers in her school during the acrimonious strikes over community control of schooling in New York in 1968–69. These strikes bitterly divided teachers and heightened racial tensions in the city for many years to come. My colleague was a new, inexperienced teacher who very much wanted help in applying ideas she had learned in her preparation to teach. Her colleagues cut her off entirely, but she developed her connections with community activists and parents, drawing on them for sustenance and assistance. She established a cordial working relationship with one other teacher, with whom she ate lunch and discussed teaching. Perhaps because of her close relations with parents and community activists, my colleague weathered the hostility and had a gratifying career as a city teacher.

I think this solution would have been less workable in many urban high schools because they are much more isolated from parents and neighborhoods. However, because high schools are generally larger than grammar or middle schools, the teaching pool is larger, so new teachers in high schools stand a greater chance of finding a few empathetic and helpful colleagues.

The Teachers Union

In urban school districts, except those in southern states that prohibit the practice, when you become a teacher you automatically have the equivalent of union dues deducted from your salary. Union membership is optional, but your paycheck will have deducted from it that portion of union dues that the union demonstrates has been spent for collective bargaining expenses. The rationale for the laws that permit this practice, called deduction of an "agency fee," is that all teachers benefit from the contract the union negotiates and the services it offers, like filing grievances for teachers who think their contract has been violated. The class-size maximum in the union contract is an example of one service you receive; negotiations for your salary and benefits, like health care, is another.

I've written elsewhere on the subject of teacher unionism and don't have space here to explore it fully, but I do want to put in a plug for what the teachers unions should be, as opposed to the form teacher unionism takes in big-city school systems. I think if you understand the purpose and potential of the union, you may look on the union differently.

Schools are workplaces, and as in most workplaces that are divided between supervisors and workers, the two groups see issues differently. In wealthy suburban school districts teachers are treated with considerably more dignity and respect than they are in city schools. They consider themselves professionals and are treated that way by the school system. For instance, the school year opened in Bedford Hills, a wealthy suburb of New York where I taught after moving from California, with a catered reception for new faculty. We met the district administrators, who had read our resumes and were acquainted with our background, and discussed educational issues.

My initiation as an employee of the New York City Board of Education began at the board's office in Brooklyn, where I was assigned an identification number and finger-printed. There was absolutely no pretense that I was a professional or that there was anything special or valuable about me as a teacher. Like the secretaries and cooks, teachers punched in and out of school on a time clock, a practice that continued until the union negotiated another procedure for recording teachers' work schedules not too long ago. Teachers in urban schools are treated like other city workers, and they have no illusions that the system appreciates them or considers them special by virtue of their education, skills, or talents.

One of the primary reasons that teacher unionism was born and reborn in city schools is that city teachers simply can't think of themselves as professionals because of the way they're treated. Every minute and action is subject to regulation. If you come late to school, your salary is docked, though it's not increased if you stay late voluntarily every day to tutor students. You're subjected to one indignity after another, like being told to fill out forms three different ways because offices downtown won't pool information. You're subjected to a barrage of insulting and nonsensical directives and forms. One of my favorites was the Board of Education's response to the first news reports about students with AIDS and the risk of contaminated blood. All New York City teachers were issued rubber gloves and directed to put them on whenever students bled; we were ordered to wash with hot, soapy water immediately after treating the injury. Yet few city schools have bathrooms for faculty or students with hot water or soap—or toilet paper for that matter, let alone paper towels.

Many teachers view the union as irrelevant to their teaching and pay little attention to its affairs. Some see the union as a barrier to school improvement. Although I understand why they feel this way, their response saddens me because I know from my experience that the teachers union can defend teachers' professional interests and at the same time be a force for progressive change in schools. When I began my teaching career in Hayward, California, I helped build our local teachers union, which recruited many of the district's teachers most interested in curriculum reform. We were active in the union because it was a vehicle for us to influence policies that affected us professionally. We monitored how the district spent its funds and publicized expenditures we considered wasteful; we demanded—and won—staff participation in planning professional development activities; we organized parents to help us hold down class size; and we struggled for well-deserved salary increases. The teachers union had excellent relations with minority parents because of our active support of community and labor struggles.

For most city teachers—and parents, too—it's hard to imagine that teachers unions can be dynamic, democratic, and progressive. But they can be! The union should be your voice, exposing the system's problems and organizing parents and citizens to join with teachers to improve conditions. Unfortunately, urban teacher unions have become bureaucratic themselves, and in the largest cities, the union leadership is removed from the concerns of the teachers. "The union" has become something separate from its members, so that school people, teachers and administrators alike, say "The union doesn't permit that," although the union contract is approved (or rejected) by a vote of the union membership and negotiated by officers who are elected and paid by union members.

In most urban schools the union has little presence, and no one wants to be elected "building rep," or union representative, because it's a great deal of work that offers minimal rewards, usually a small amount of time out of the classroom and perhaps a token financial reimbursement. The building rep funnels information from the union leadership to members and meets with the principal about issues of concern to the faculty. However, in schools that have weak union chapters, the union's existence is felt mostly at the district level and through provisions in the contract the union leadership negotiates. For these reasons, unless you make a special effort to become involved in the union, it will be a shadowy presence in your professional life.

Even if you can't see yourself becoming active in the union to improve it, you should attend the union meetings held in your school and become acquainted with the building rep. Both are important sources of information for you. I hate to say this, but I must—in many urban schools the building rep is not a person who is considered an exceptional teacher, though he or she is almost never someone who is incompetent. There's often a division between teachers who take care of union affairs and those who focus on curriculum and teaching, although in my experience the most effective building reps are those who are highly respected as teachers. Still, many times your building rep can help you when you run into barriers in trying to do a better job of teaching. The advice my building rep gave me about how to handle the coats-in-class rule illustrates the kind of guidance your building rep can provide. Even building reps who are not themselves stellar instructors can give you information that will help you to become one, by learning how to circumvent regulations without defying supervisors and imperiling your position.

Some new teachers who have not had experience with unions may be afraid that they will be scrutinized by administrators if they go to union meetings or have contact with the building rep. This is almost never the case in urban schools, where the union's presence is accepted without question. Can you trust that concerns you express to the building rep will be kept in confidence, as they should be? A building rep would almost never reveal confidential information because his or her credibility with the teachers would be lost, and with it the ability to influence relations between the staff and administration. In schools with terrible working conditions and a totally demoralized staff, you may find a building rep who is more interested in currying favor with administrators than helping colleagues, and then you're stuck. If you remain in the school until you're tenured, your only choice is to work with like-minded colleagues to take over the union by voting in a new building rep, perhaps yourself—after you're tenured.

It can be hard to see the potential for teachers unions in urban school systems because the unions are so stale, so fixed on maintaining the status quo. But all kinds of unions throughout the country, in fact all over the world, are in crisis right now, and teachers unions are no exception. They can't figure out how to respond to the drastically changed political and economic landscape, and the demands being made on education. The generation of teachers entering urban schools now will have to provide a new direction for teacher unionism if teachers are going to influence life in their schools. And nowhere is this more important than in urban school districts, where teachers are the single most stable, powerful institutional constituency for improving education.

Though urban teachers unions are lethargic, relatively conservative, and bureaucratic, the officers are directly elected. A few urban school systems have seen the entrenched union leaders defeated by reform groups, who have restored public confidence in the teaching staff by advocating progressive change. If new teachers become involved in the union to make it fight for their ideas about improving schools, they can make teacher unionism a partner in the social movement that's needed to improve urban schools. Classroom teachers have to demand more of their unions to transform them from the dues-collecting machines they've become.

6 Your Students

The question of whether children in urban classrooms are different from kids elsewhere has been a source of contention in educational research and policy for the past hundred years. It's an important issue because the starting point for our decisions about how we teach should be judgments of who our students are. Although I think that we can't fully understand how teachers and students behave in schools without taking into account school structures and policies, teachers and students bring differing knowledge, abilities, and beliefs that affect how they function in the classroom.

When I wrote my other book on urban teacher preparation, I was so concerned about shifting the focus of researchers from the characteristics of teachers and students to the conditions in urban schools, that I didn't try to analyze whether kids in urban schools are different in any way from their counterparts in the suburbs. However, in rethinking my own experience, I realize that my students in the city schools were different from those I had worked with in the suburbs.

In Chapters 1 and 2 I discussed the concept of a continuum to explain that "urban-ness" shouldn't be considered an either/or situation. I think the same holds true of students who've been raised in cities; they differ from their counterparts in the suburbs in ways that have to do with the distinctive aspects of city life. When I taught in Malverne and Bedford Hills, two small suburbs of New York City, I noticed that teenagers who had only recently moved to these suburbs were more sophisticated and had an edge, an energy, that their suburban classmates lacked. In Bedford Hills, the students who had newly emigrated were white, the children of well-educated professionals who had lived in Manhattan's prosperous sections. In Malverne, the students were usually sons and daughters of African American civil servants who had lived in working-class, segregated communities in Brooklyn and Queens. In both situations, the suburban students and I saw differences in their expectations and behavior that were clearly a result of their having lived in city neighborhoods.

I think these differences make sense because teachers and students bring attitudes and behaviors to school that they've acquired in living in particular places, and cities are no different from other locales in making their mark on the way we view life and respond to it. Kids who are raised in neighborhoods where the harshness of life is immediately apparent, as it is in poor communities, are often used to defending themselves verbally and physically. If their families have had negative experiences with intrusive governmental agencies, they may be very concerned about their privacy and withhold information you request in order to help them. If they are used to hearing people speak their minds bluntly, they will expect to respond this way to you and their classmates.

I've heard people describe city kids as being "street smart," in contrast to being "school smart." I really dislike that characterization because it implies that the astuteness and maturity that children have developed by living in a demanding environment aren't applicable to the learning that should occur in school. When teachers are knowledgeable and respectful about the ways city life can support their efforts to teach, "street smart" is simply "smart."

Applying Information About Cultural Differences

I've found the existing scholarship on urban teacher preparation to be of little help in assisting new teachers because it's missed what I think is a central point: Even if the student population in urban schools is distinctive, students' characteristics can't be understood in isolation from the conditions in urban schools. For this reason one thread of research on urban schools—scholarship identifying important variations in the ways different groups accommodate to the rigid, impersonal character of urban schools—is especially helpful to teachers when it is used wisely. However, this research has to be used as background information, not as a formula that predicts the behavior and performance of students. Moreover, it shouldn't be used, as it sometimes is, to blame children and parents for academic failure, thereby justifying the educational system's historic and contemporary failure to provide all children with a high-quality education. Applying knowledge about cultural differences to teaching is perplexing because people are members of many different categories and groups. They may share a nationality but hold to different religions, be considered members of the same racial category but come from different class backgrounds, share the same language but differ in gender and sexual orientation. Many teachers are wary of using information about cultural differences because they see how easily it leads to stereotyping, to robbing people of their individuality. However, their response that "Kids are kids" ignores significant political, economic, and social forces that influence school success.

Much has been written about the role of culture in school achievement, and you should be knowledgeable about this scholarship. More often than not, the media present a superficial, sensationalized version of scholarly debates about the effects of culture on academic success, so if your acquaintance with this topic is based primarily on conversations with friends, your own impressions, and the popular media, you need to educate yourself by reading in more depth or taking an intellectually serious course. Not all college courses that have "multicultural education" in the title will give you the background you need to think through the topic. In fact, one researcher found that workshops given to new teachers in Los Angeles didn't change their teaching practice at all and, for some, actually increased the tendency to think about students stereotypically. I think an ideal course acquaints you with key scholarship and helps you to think about the role of culture and its components—like race, religion, and gender—in education generally and in your personal academic history.

I should clarify what I mean when I use the word *culture* because the word has two definitions—"culture" in the anthropological sense and also as a synonym for "civilization" or "erudition." "Culture" to anthropologists is the meaning a group of people assign to events and objects in their lives; in this definition, "culture" is not limited to people who are well educated. Everyone who talks and socializes with other people is part of a "culture."

One idea that my students have found helpful in making sense of social distinctions is to understand that many of the differences that we take for granted are "socially constructed." At a particular time and place, societies give biologically apparent variations among people different meanings. For instance, many groups that we call "nationalities" today, like Italians, were called "races" at the turn of the last century. In this country we identify skin color as a determinant of race, but this definition is not universal. We can identify biological differences between males and females, but what these differences imply about the way we view our ourselves has changed a great deal from the time I began my teaching career. In the interview for my first teaching job at age 22, the superintendent, an older man who was a nationally recognized educator, asked me "Why is it that such an attractive young lady isn't married?" At that point, women were just starting to challenge the social construction of gender that defined women through their roles as mothers and wives, so the superintendent's question was logical—to him.

Because we are immersed in our own culture, we take it for granted and often forget that we bring to all our social interactions a particular cultural frame of reference that has not been shared by all people at all times. If you've traveled to foreign countries or spots in the United States that differ significantly from your home territory, you've probably been struck by cultural variations. When I have the opportunity, I enjoy browsing through guidebooks written in other languages for foreign visitors to New York City because they present so many aspects of city life differently from the way I'm used to viewing it. One guidebook written for French travelers on a budget warns its readers that in U.S. restaurants you'll be considered rude if you ask for "the toilet." Due to our Puritan background, we say "bathroom" or "restroom," the book cautions, rather than the straightforward "w.c." (water closet) or "toilette" used in France. The book pokes fun at our laws prohibiting drinking beer and wine in public areas, like parks or street benches, because the French treat wine like we do soft drinks.

Using knowledge about cultural differences while avoiding stereotypes requires that teachers regard information about cultural differences in the same way that competent doctors use epidemiological data. They keep it in the back of their mind to inform their decisions, but they don't automatically make it the diagnosis. A chest pain in a man who's a member of group that's at high risk for heart disease might be caused by indigestion from a chili dog, or it might indicate a heart attack. We'd expect the doctor to question and examine the patient as part of the process of making a diagnosis, using information from clinical observation along with his or her knowledge of the risk factors for heart disease among different groups.

The same process occurs in classrooms. Your knowledge of cultural factors is by itself an inadequate basis for making instructional decisions, yet data about cultural differences will often be useful. Because conditions in urban school systems pressure you to treat your students as an undifferentiated mass, you'll find that the more information you have about your students' backgrounds, the better equipped you are to deal with them as individuals. Knowing that a student is Muslim, that observant Muslims don't eat from sunup to sundown during Ramadan, and that Ramadan falls at a certain time of year doesn't necessarily explain why your student is sleeping in class, but it suggests explanations that you'll want to consider.

The more information you can tap about students' lives outside school, the more efficient you'll become in developing hypotheses and solutions in your teaching. How can you acquire this data? The starting point should be an acknowledgment that your own experiences, expectations, and values are not necessarily generalizable to your students. You'll miss important cues that you should pursue when students express their ideas if you aren't alert to the information you're receiving. In this regard, you need to consider yourself an anthropologist, putting aside many of your ideas about how people should and do act, seeking alternative explanations for your students' behavior and thinking. In suggesting that you think as an anthropologist, I need to clarify that you seek this information in order to learn from your students, not study them as research subjects.

One of the characteristics of urban school systems I described in Chapter 1 is that they serve a highly diverse group of students. If you are like most new, young teachers, learning to work with students and parents who are culturally different from yourself is a significant challenge. I use the term "culturally different" because in urban schools especially, all teachers face students who are culturally different from themselves, though the extent of difference varies according to the setting and the teacher. For example, if you are a white, middle-class teacher who is an English monolingual working with poor and working-class Chinese children, the gulf in life experience between you and your students will probably be quite substantial and made more so by language differences. If you are a mature, upper-middle-class African American who has changed careers and you teach poor and working-class African American and Chicano students, your students will be culturally different from you, but the dissimilarities you experience may seem to be a by-product of factors other than race, like class or generational differences. Teachers raised and educated in the same neighborhood as their students often have an overlapping cultural frame, but even here their experiences of the community may differ in significant ways. Though raised in the same neighborhood, they may have seen it differently because of their family's structure, values, and economic position.

If you use scholarship about culture as background information wisely—for instance, that done by the anthropologist John Ogbu— research can help you make sense of how these cultural differences may influence school achievement. As mentioned in Chapter 2, Ogbu distinguishes between students who are "voluntary" minorities, who have emigrated to this country voluntarily for political or economic reasons, and those belonging to "involuntary" minorities, whose presence is due to their subjugation, either as a colonized people or as slaves. Although both kinds of minorities face discrimination, especially if they are dark-skinned or speak another language, they respond differently because of their disparate cultural frames of reference. To voluntary minorities, discrimination and poverty are obstacles to be bypassed; for involuntary minorities, instances of oppression are often experienced as examples of their permanently subordinate status, reminders that they will never be allowed to be equal.

Even if you teach in a school that seems to be homogeneous—for instance, a racially isolated school serving African American or Spanish-speaking immigrants—you will find that these categories obscure equally meaningful cultural variations. At King High School, I initially taught African American students who were born-and-bred New Yorkers, as well as students recently arrived in Harlem from small towns in the rural South. After I had taught for 2 years at King, the city altered its policy on admission to neighborhood high schools, and students from Jamaica and the U.S. Virgin Islands enrolled because King was safer than their neighborhood schools in Brooklyn. As a group they differed in their attitudes about school and teachers as much from the native New Yorkers as they did from one another. Similarly, Dominican, Puerto Rican, and Colombian students leaving the bilingual program all spoke Spanish but brought to the mainstream classes very different educational backgrounds and aspirations.

When we analyze Ogbu's work in my graduate classes, many teachers tell me that his distinction helps to explain why so many immigrant students who come from poor, uneducated families do well in urban schools while their classmates who were born in this country languish. The distinction helps explain why Puerto Rican students may be more ambivalent about learning English than classmates who are recent arrivals from Ecuador. For Puerto Rican students, English is the language of the colonizing power; they may feel that they are relinquishing their self-respect if they speak the language of the culture that dominates them. Historically Ecuador has had a different relationship with the United States, and Ecuadorian immigrants view acquiring English differently, regarding it as their passport to an improved life. The phenomenon is international: In Scandinavia, Finns, who are involuntary minorities, fare poorly in school; in Australia, where both groups are voluntary minorities, Finnish and Scandinavian immigrants do equally well.

You can understand from Ogbu's framework why the behavior of a white, middle-class teacher may be suspect in the eyes of involuntary minorities, especially in schools that have few faculty or administrators who share the cultural background of the students. The teacher's higher social and economic status, and position in a school system that for most of its existence legally and openly discriminated against racial minorities, can make teachers appear to be supporters of the status quo, even if they are not. I think that in order to persuade your students and their parents that students will benefit from what you and the school can offer, you must acknowledge the validity of their cultural framework while helping them, if they wish, to adapt to the dominant culture. Generally speaking, you can win their confidence by making intellectual and social space in your classroom for cultural differences, acknowledging that all students bring life experiences, beliefs, and ideas that are no less worthy of examination than your own or those of classmates.

An intellectual understanding of the distinction between voluntary and involuntary minorities has helped many of the teachers in my classes make sense of the contradictory ways their students respond to the demands of school. I have to insert a cautionary note here, however, because I regularly encounter teachers who ignore Ogbu's emphasis on the dynamic interaction between racism, as a continuing problem, and the response of involuntary minorities to it. For instance, Frank, a new high school biology teacher in a school with a large black student population, wrote in one assignment for my class that he lauded Ogbu's work because it supported the observation that he and his colleagues made in their lunchtime discussions: The problems of black students were of their own making; they just didn't take advantage of all the opportunities the school afforded them.

No, no, no! When I receive responses like Frank's, I question whether I should present Ogbu's work because it is criticized for encouraging teachers from the majority culture to blame involuntary minorities for school failure. I see a point in this criticism; however, I suggest you use Ogbu's work because I think his ideas are valuable. Still, responses like Frank's highlight that teachers need more than data about cultural differences and racism; they also must have a willingness to examine their own cultural frame of reference, an ability to be "open," one of the attributes of reflective teaching.

For many of the new teachers I work with, Ogbu's framework helps them understand the source of the seemingly unprovoked hostility involuntary minorities may bring to school. It helps them to move beyond their own anger to make their classroom more accessible to all students. Frank, Rosanna, and Claudine, beginning teachers enrolled in my graduate course at the College of Staten Island on issues in urban education, exemplify how the ability to apply research on cultural differences depends on "openness."

When we analyzed Ogbu's work, Rosanna, a young, white second-year teacher who taught in a city grammar school serving many poor African American families, echoed Frank's anger at black families. She expressed outrage that one of the third-graders in her class insisted that blacks "can't trust white people." Rosanna argued that the remark was evidence of parents creating racial hostility that undercut her authority. However, a classmate disagreed with Rosanna's analysis, calling attention to news accounts of racism, like a brawl that started when two young children were called "dirty little niggers" by a city bus driver. Throughout the course Rosanna held to her belief that many of the African American parents fomented racial discord by discussing racial differences with their children. Rosanna's response to Ogbu's work was that by placing the academic performance of involuntary minorities in a historical, social, and political context, it "excused" the behavior and attitude of students who were not taking advantage of what the public school system had to offer.

In my view, although Rosanna was intelligent, dedicated, and hard-working, she was in danger of becoming like the alienated teachers she disliked. Because she was not open to viewing her school and herself as involuntary minorities might perceive them, she couldn't see that her students' life experiences might give them a perspective on race and schooling that, however upsetting to her, was consistent with their circumstances. Despite her professed affection for her students, Rosanna probably communicated her anger to those students who did not share her beliefs about race. Inadvertently, she buttressed the mistrust the parents of some of her African American students had for her, white teachers, and the school.

In contrast, another novice teacher in my class, Claudine—like Rosanna a young, white Staten Island resident—described to me how acquiring the ability to identify her own cultural frame of reference had totally altered the way she viewed her relations with students and parents, as well as her teaching. Although she had not begun her teaching career with this attitude, Claudine now considered cultural differences in the classroom an asset because they presented her with opportunities to learn about herself, her teaching, and life. In one of her assignments toward the end of the semester, Claudine recalled an incident that occurred when she had just begun teaching, in a Head Start program serving poor, African American children. "I was very confident, nurturing, energetic, and professional at 20 years of age," she noted, and the director and parents frequently complimented her on her teaching ability. Claudine had worked with a teacher's assistant and described the incident she had recently reconsidered:

> She was a Creole woman from the South, about 50 years of age, who was very lively and nurturing to the children. We worked well as a team. However, one day everything changed. I led the children out to the lunchroom where she had prepared their morning snack, sliced peaches in heavy syrup with a cup of milk. This was not my planned snack. "Milk would be too heavy with peaches in syrup. It will make their tummies sick," I said to her.
>
> "No, it will not," she answered. I became short with her. "I wrote juice for the menu. My mother always served me water or

juice with this canned fruit. I feel safer serving juice to the children." At this point, she stated, "Well, where I'm from in Tennessee, my mamma served us peaches and cream. We never got sick. You see, I was raised on it. You're narrow in your cultural experience. You need to see other ways of life." I was humiliated and disgusted with this woman.

The conflict between Claudine and her assistant escalated, as the woman introduced "dolls, dances, and songs from her childhood." Consequently the assistant was removed from the room, and Claudine and she "rarely spoke again."

After describing the incident, Claudine analyzed how her opinion about it had changed. The important issue was not peaches and milk: The woman might have been right about the snack, or she might have been wrong. What was most critical was that Claudine had been unable to see that the aide, notwithstanding her lack of formal education, could provide her with information and insights that would help Claudine be a better teacher. She noted that a tremendous weight was lifted from her shoulders when she realized that she didn't have to know everything and could learn from her students and their parents. Claudine's new stance changed her self-conception as a teacher. Instead of being the expert, she was now a self-confident explorer, poised to pursue new interpretations of the curriculum—and life.

Judy, a new teacher in Brooklyn, explained how pivotal the teacher's attitude towards cultural differences is, contrasting her own performance in two schools. She had been teaching in a predominantly white, middle class elementary school in Brooklyn, where the majority of students were third and fourth generation Italian-Americans, like herself. Parents were active in their children's schooling, and students were competitive and highly motivated. Then the student population began to change, with Chinese, Russian, and Pakistani students attending. Judy explained:

> I found myself becoming impatient with this change. Academically, these children were not performing like the majority population of the school. The teachers, including myself, were having difficulty meeting and understanding their needs. I was guilty of taking on the attitudes of my peers, instead of developing my own. Teaching was getting harder and we didn't have the necessary resources to make it any easier.

Then she was transferred to another school, 30 blocks away, where students from the former Yugoslavia, China, Puerto Rico, India, and Russia, were the majority in the school. She realized that "my students were the resources all along. They come equipped with all the tools," but teachers have to know how to use them. Proudly, Judy wrote:

> For the past 5 months, my students have taught me how to educate them. They come to me with their own cultural experiences. We, as a class, laugh, discuss, and at times share so many emotions, such as tears, as we share our personal experiences.

Judy brings students' parents and family members to share their experiences and invited her own father to speak about his work on the Apollo space program. Teaching in this new way has completely altered her orientation as a teacher. "I stand before them changed," she observed.

A colleague who read an earlier draft of this book cautioned me that Judy's quote that students bring the "tools" they need to succeed might make the task of acquiring proficiency in a new language seem automatic, as if students can easily learn English on their own. Au contraire! Anyone who's tried to become literate in a second language knows how arduous it is! The notion that we can plop students into English-speaking classes and expect them to master English—the sink-or-swim philosophy—is simply wrong for many kinds of children. I can't explore issues in second-language learning in this book with the seriousness they deserve because there's not room, but you should know that teachers certainly need to acquire knowledge about the process of second-language learning so that they can assist their students. They need to know, for example, how to tap the strength of the student's oral base in his or her native language. When Judy wrote that she saw that her students had the "tools" they needed to learn, I think she recognized that they bring skills and knowledge, cognitive and affective abilities, that teachers should use. One of those abilities is their linguistic strength in their native language. There are many, many others.

The Teacher as Learner

I think that the most successful urban teachers regard their students as people from whom they have much to learn as well as much to teach. They and their students regard the classroom as a community or family in which everyone's talents and abilities are respected. Though this stance toward teaching is valuable in classrooms everywhere, it is most difficult to sustain and most essential in urban schools because of the impersonal, anonymous, over-regulated environment.

In most urban schools teachers have little or no input about who is placed in their classes; the curriculum may be mandated, and even if the teacher's compliance is not monitored directly, students' performance on standardized tests is frequently used as a measure of the teacher's effectiveness. Especially in the most dysfunctional schools, the materials and textbooks available are those purchased by administrators at a central office without teacher or parent input; more often than not teachers find these books inappropriate for students in their classes. For example, in elementary schools in an urban district in New Jersey that had been taken over by the state, each teacher had to use expensive new texts from a math series that the district's teacher advisory committee had recommended against purchasing.

The incessant pressure to cover predetermined material with students whose abilities and interests vary immensely encourages authoritarian teaching behaviors and custodial treatment of students. To resist these constraints, I think urban teachers need, first and foremost, the expectation that they are capable of helping their students to succeed academically. I know that in many teacher education courses the role of expectations is expressed differently; what's emphasized is that the teacher must have high expectations for all students. But in my discussions with my students who have completed their student teaching in urban schools in New Jersey, we've decided that the issue of expectations is much more complex. Students bring expectations about themselves and about teachers, and vice versa. What's critical is that teachers be confident of their ability to teach and communicate their confidence and determination to all students.

In addition to this attitude, city teachers need to be especially skillful in three aspects of curriculum and instruction. First, they should be knowledgeable about a broad range of teaching strategies, because they teach children with such a vast assortment of needs. Second, they need to understand the content they teach well enough to ferret out the essence, so that they can help students master content that seems arcane, irrelevant, and remote. Third, they need to create a sense of community in their classrooms. I think that really fine teachers everywhere are competent in these areas, but for urban teachers to be even moderately effective with all of their students, they must be well-skilled in all three realms.

I don't think that successful urban teachers are necessarily extraordinary in all three areas, and they don't have to be because a strength in one domain can compensate for relative weakness in another. I've seen teachers who are less knowledgeable than others about content, who prepare lessons that aren't intrinsically motivating to students; but these teachers do such a fine job of creating community spirit and trust that their students do what's expected of them, even if they aren't especially interested in the material. Sometimes teachers can draw on students' expectations that because they come from the neighborhood and are of the same race or culture, they'll be more understanding and committed. You still have to be able find ways to make the curriculum accessible, but you have an important asset that a teacher who's perceived differently doesn't. On the other hand, when I taught at Julia Richman and Martin Luther King, Jr., High School, I worked with many African American students who viewed me suspiciously, expecting that I couldn't and wouldn't try to understand them or appreciate them. I think that my ability to create lessons that showed my students the power of their own ideas, lessons that connected instruction to their life experiences and validated it, helped me overcome the students' initial expectations about me as an older white teacher.

Much of the current talk about school reform, about helping all children master high standards, stresses the shift from viewing teachers as people who transmit knowledge to another perspective—the teacher as leader of a classroom of learners. In this model, teachers learn from and with their students while maintaining responsibility for the orderly functioning of the classroom. This kind of teaching is immensely difficult but critical in urban schools because it establishes a dynamic between you and your students that is exactly the opposite of the relationship that the school system's bureaucratic nature pressures you to adopt. When you set up your classroom so that students respect and learn from one another, and you learn from them, you contradict the hierarchical nature of the school system. When you use teaching strategies that call for your students to interpret and analyze material so that you and they critically compare ideas, you counter the "skill–drill–kill" sort of instruction that lends itself to the test-driven curricula that characterize many urban schools.

Including All Students

Both the difficulty and necessity of creating classrooms that are communities have become more acute in the years since I left high school teaching in 1990; today urban teachers work in classrooms containing students with an even greater span of abilities. Because of changes in immigration, classrooms contain significant numbers of students who know little or no English, who receive instruction in ESL, or English as a Second Language, in pull-out programs. For 45 minutes the student is tutored, usually with other children pulled from other classes, but for most of the school day this student, who may speak no English, is in the regular classroom.

The other change that has accelerated since I left teaching in the city schools is a policy of integrating children in special education programs into regular classrooms. "Inclusion" or "Integration" programs, as they are called, vary enormously from one school to another, but they all result in regular classrooms containing students with disabilities who were previously taught only in special education classes.

These changes underscore the need for urban teachers to become masterful in the three areas I mentioned above: making the classroom a community, understanding the subject matter thoroughly, and employing a broad range of teaching strategies. With some digging you'll find excellent resources to assist you in each of these areas, but I want to stress one technique that has helped me in all three realms—cooperative learning.

I think that learning to use small groups well is a key skill for urban teachers for a number of reasons. Small-group work *when it is done correctly* makes students more responsible for their own learning; it empowers them within your classroom. Helping students to regulate their behavior and analyze their own learning is a considerable challenge in urban schools because the school structure and working conditions encourage teachers to be the boss, to treat their students in a custodial fashion. Students' normal desire to interact, which is usually stymied in the name of academic achievement, is channeled for the same end when they work in small groups. When students interact in a well-structured small-group activity that requires language, students who have varying abilities teach one another language skills as well as content knowledge. I stress that small-group work needs to be carefully planned because if it is not done well, it can reinforce status inequalities among children. Please don't think using small groups is simply a matter of having the students push their seats together! Learning to use small groups is a skill that has to be mastered.

Many city kids have adult responsibilities outside school, but in the classroom they are infantilized, denied control or power over what they do. This struck me one day when I observed a 9-year-old boy in a Manhattan park, playing and minding his 2-year-old brother for several hours, as I watched my young daughter. Concerned about this young boy, I asked him if he was in the park alone, and he told me that his mom was in their apartment, down the block but out of sight and earshot of the park. Later I heard him discussing with his classmates how much he hated school, and I thought about the contrast between his freedom out of school and his confinement in the classroom. I wondered at the enormous self-discipline he would have to show in most classrooms, where his behavior and language would be continually scrutinized by a teacher. Small-group work helps a child like this to taste within the classroom's four walls a bit of the independence that he has out of school.

Another reason to master use of cooperative learning is to help students who are not native speakers of English learn both the new language and the regular curriculum. Small-group work provides far more opportunities for kids to express themselves in a low-risk setting. They have a chance to practice English with native speakers, something they may not do outside of school. Whole class instruction simply doesn't give them the chance to use their new language frequently enough and in enough different ways. In addition, the anonymous, impersonal atmosphere of the urban school can be alienating to students who come from cultures in which teachers know and are familiar with families; small-group work, by helping students to develop relationships with one another, aids them in bridging the gap between the warmth and familiarity of home and the coldness and isolation of most urban schools.

The other reason I encourage you to learn how to use small groups well with your students is that when it is used correctly, it alters your students' relations with one another. Urban schools, especially the high schools, are frequently large and anonymous. Just as you don't have an opportunity to get to know your students if your contact with them is limited to your being in front of the class feeding them information, they won't have an opportunity to become acquainted with one another and develop the social and language skills people need to collaborate. We know from research that small-group work is the single most effective strategy teachers can use to promote better intergroup relations among students, in the classroom specifically and in the school generally. One bonus of well-planned small groups is that they free up a few minutes for teachers to work with students individually. In the large classes that are common in urban schools, teachers have no time to work with students singly, unless they find a way to create it.

In the years I've been supervising student teachers I've encountered many teachers who tell me that group work may work for some students, perhaps those in the honors classes or the suburbs, but for "these kids," it's not an effective method of instruction. Invariably, when good teachers learn how to use small groups correctly, they become converts. Opposition to small-group work frequently arises when the teacher has not known how to use the small-group configuration appropriately, often because the students have not been taught the social and language skills they need to work in groups. We're not born knowing how to collaborate; we acquire the knowledge and ability, either directly through instruction, or indirectly by observing and modeling behavior, or both. To use cooperative learning effectively, teachers have to analyze what academic and social skills their students need to know to accomplish the tasks set out for them. Then teachers have to teach these skills, just as they do content.

Small groups can be used to help students analyze "hot" topics without the risk that's incurred in commenting on a controversial issue in front of the entire class. Discussing racial, religious, and gender divisions in urban schools is especially difficult because teachers aren't given any institutional support for this tricky business. Although each of the three city high schools I taught in was troubled by racial or ethnic divisions, among both staff and students, the schools never addressed the problems openly. My use of small groups helped students to become sufficiently acquainted and comfortable with one another that we could discuss racial tensions without the explosions that I and other teachers feared.

Cooperative learning helps integrate special education students into the classroom for all the reasons that it's beneficial for other students. In addition, when students are working with one another in well-planned small-group activities, you have a chance to circulate among the groups, providing extra assistance to students who require it. Many times your "special needs" students won't require help from you because their peers provide it—and benefit in the process, both socially and intellectually.

Of course, there are other valuable teaching strategies that you need to learn, because you need to have a wide range of instructional alternatives at your fingertips. And I have to admit that I do know a few teachers who are highly respected and admired among students, faculty, and administrators whose classrooms are entirely teacher-directed, who don't use cooperative learning. They transmit their great love of learning and their respect for each student as an individual to the class through their powerful personalities; the students absorb these notions and use the teacher's behavior, language, and attitudes as models for their own. However, for each teacher who succeeds brilliantly using an exclusive diet of whole-class instruction, I can point to 20 who don't. Moreover, there's no way we can duplicate the success of these remarkably talented teachers, except by cloning their personalities, whereas almost everyone can learn how to use small groups well.

Knowing the Subject Matter

The other indispensable ability for urban teachers is understanding their subject matter well enough to examine it from different perspectives. Here again the proficiency is one all teachers should have but urban teachers *must* have if they are going to be successful. When you are given a curriculum you have to follow or a textbook you must use, you need to know the subject well enough so that you can filter out the essence of the material and then use your knowledge of teaching to present the concept or skill so that it's meaningful to your students. One of my student teachers described this process as being able to "walk around" the material, seeing it from other perspectives, understanding its essence so that he could cast it in different ways for his students.

Whether you're teaching algebra, addition, Chaucer, or geography, you need to be able to answer this question: "Why am I teaching this content to these students?" If your response is that "It's in the curriculum" or "It's in the textbook" or "They need it for fifth grade," you've avoided your obligation to develop a personal understanding of the value of the content. Without a personal sense of the relevance of the material you're supposed to teach, you won't be able to discover ways of making it meaningful to your students, so you'll be chained to an instructional routine that emphasizes rote learning and low-level cognitive skills. If the material is boring to you, you haven't a chance to make it motivating for your students. As I discuss in the next chapter, creating high-quality lessons is the key to having your classroom function well; understanding what's of value in the content you demand that your students master is a key to planning effective lessons.

Sometimes you must ask your students to study material that has little redeeming value other than its probable presence on a standardized test that affects their careers and yours as well. In New York State all students must pass a battery of tests to graduate, and if teachers don't help students pass these tests, they're not fulfilling their obligations. However, if students have thrived for much of the year on stimulating content, they will usually stay focused for short intervals on boring material they have to learn. In my experience, being frank about the reasons for covering this content, separating it from the important (to me) work that we do but conveying its value in practical terms, helps students to accept an unappealing learning task. But in order to ask students to master content that they find irrelevant and boring, you need to have helped them to trust you and to have experienced a different kind of learning. To accomplish that end, you need to understand your students and the content you're teaching well enough to construct lessons that are motivating.

This task is more difficult in some subjects and some schools than others. Much depends on the degree to which content is controlled by forces outside your classroom. For instance, math curricula are often highly regulated and taught sequentially. If kids don't master a skill or concept at a particular moment, they'll be lost in the subsequent material. In situations like this your ability to present concepts in many different ways is critical; your room to manipulate *what* you're teaching is quite limited, so you have to search for alternative roads to understand the same material.

During an interview I conducted with student teachers a few years ago for a research project, one of them, Kelly, who had a class that was difficult, but not exceptionally so, commented that in one way her education classes had led her astray. She remarked that "you learn to do a little of this, a little of that, and throw in some group work, and everything will be fine. But actually the kids are bouncing off of the walls and you don't know what to do! Nothing seems to work!" Kelly's criticism comes to my mind as I conclude this section because I think that I may have made the job of teaching in an urban school seem far easier than it is.

I haven't meant to imply that the ideas I've presented are recipes that will eliminate the intense frustrations and disappointments that are an inevitable aspect of your life in the urban classroom. As an antidote to that impression, I'll acknowledge that in my sixth year of teaching in the city, I had a freshman English class after lunch that was impossible for me teach. It wasn't an especially large group, but it contained several young men who were 18 and 19 and visited class a day or two every few weeks, as well as a core of typical 14-year-olds, including four who had significant difficulties with English. I spent about half of every period reprimanding students for throwing books, screaming insults at one another, or grabbing some body part of a classmate. Just as I'd have some success in handling the 14-year-olds, one of the older students would come to class, completely out of the loop. I consulted counselors, the department head, revised the curriculum. Frankly, it was hell, and I said things to students I regretted as soon as the words left my mouth.

I've thought many times about that class, guiltily, trying to figure out what I could have done differently. I think the only way that I could have saved that class was by tracking down each of the students who attended irregularly and developing an entirely individual course of study. But even that might not have worked because they missed whole weeks of all their classes, not only mine, so I'd have had to find something that was powerful enough to bring them to school, not just my class.

We all have those classes, those days, or those weeks. In the next chapter I analyze the special problems of classroom management in urban schools because I think that information will help you to reduce the number of times you feel like you'd rather be anywhere else, *anywhere*, but your classroom. Still, Kelly's final words remind us why, even after a class from hell, we stick it out and try harder.

"And then," she said, "you do something right and they learn. And you can see that they appreciate it. And there's no better feeling in the world."

7 Managing Your Classroom

If you're anxious about making your students do what you tell them to do, you're typical of most prospective and beginning teachers. "Discipline" and "class control" are often the greatest concerns novice teachers have, especially those who have not worked in schools in other capacities or supervised others. Young teachers going into urban schools who have not lived in the communities their school serves can be more anxious about their role as the class leader because their life experiences haven't prepared them for the role. In fact, their unfamiliarity with their students as people is a major hurdle to becoming comfortable and skillful in managing a city classroom. And though they may find admitting these feelings painful, in all honesty they have to acknowledge that they are fearful of their students and the setting.

I see this fear when I tell many educated, white, middle-class people who have no personal contact with urban schools or minority children that I help prepare teachers for city schools. The response is frequently a jocular comment about whether I'm an expert on self-defense or use of lethal weapons. I attribute the comments partly to the portrait of urban schools and their students the media conveys to the public. This information, combined with a lack of first-hand knowledge of urban classrooms and children, can heighten a prospective urban teacher's fears about violence in schools, which in turn exacerbates the usual apprehension about managing a classroom of people. We see reports of violence in schools so often that we tend to think that they are like war zones. In my experience, the reality is quite different, although there's no doubt that urban teachers deal with the threat of violent behavior more often than do their counterparts in suburbs and small towns, and they have to be more knowledgeable and skillful in managing student behavior.

To some extent urban teaching's greater demand for skill in classroom management derives from the conditions I've described in this book: Chronic shortages of materials and supplies, poor facilities, isolation from parents and community, and bureaucratic intrusions and overregulation increase the difficulty of making the classroom a community and serving students' individual needs. However, the surroundings in which city kids live also make establishing a respectful, focused classroom environment in an urban school a weighty challenge. Life in American cities, and especially the poorest neighborhoods in them, is violent and anonymous in comparison with everyday existence outside the city. When I vacation in the countryside, I'm always reminded how much survival in American cities depends on being alert to danger, and I'm struck by customs that by standards of life in the city are foolishly naive: People leave bicycles on their porches, unlocked, and farm stands are frequently left unattended, with customers trusted to leave money for the produce they take with them. When I go to restaurants in the suburbs, I often seem women leave their purses hanging on the back of the chair, which in many spots in cities is an invitation to theft.

Urban teachers have to know how to deal with the attitudes and habits that city kids acquire in their neighborhoods and homes, because students bring behaviors grounded in their lives outside school into classrooms. Life is harsh for many city children, even those who experience bountiful family love and support. I'll never forget my dismay the first time I gave students in my English classes at Martin Luther King, Jr., High School the same journal topic I had used in the suburbs, "A night I'll never forget." I was used to reading lighthearted anecdotes, tales of dates and family reunions, or perhaps a rueful recounting of an adolescent escapade that had ended with a minor punishment; on occasion a student would describe a very sad incident, like the death of a sibling or a parent. But in my classes at King the topic often generated stunning reports of friends lost to violent deaths, or one I'll never forget: A 15-year-old recalled attending the wake of her cousin, who had been killed by gunfire; what stuck in her mind was not the wake, but the theft of the gold chain from her cousin's corpse.

A great many kids in poor neighborhoods are surrounded by brutal crime, and the behavior that helps them to survive in their neighborhood often conflicts with the conduct schools and teachers demand. In a classroom we require students to replace a defensive stance and aggressive behavior with quite a different sort of conduct. We insist that they negotiate differences and rely on school authorities to protect their personal safety, rather than defending themselves. As I described earlier in the coats-in-the-classroom problem, urban schools often don't adequately safeguard students and their property. When schools and teachers demand that students follow regulations that make them vulnerable but do not create a safe environment, they inadvertently encourage children to disregard and reject the school's behavioral norms. Children often violate school rules of conduct, sacrificing their prospect of academic success, to safeguard themselves and their belongings because they do not trust authorities in schools to provide them with adequate protection. You need to make your classroom a safe haven so that your students don't have to choose between protecting themselves and their property or conforming to classroom norms.

Like most teacher educators, I don't advise you to think about the task of making your classroom orderly, safe, and productive simply in terms of disciplining students to make them do what you want or controlling their misbehavior. If you want your students to act differently in your classroom than they do on the street, you need to be sure that they and their property will be safeguarded. Moreover, all aspects of classroom life must encourage appropriate behavior and discourage conduct that makes other students feel devalued or unsafe. No matter how much or how severely you discipline students, you won't have a well-functioning classroom if the setup undercuts or contradicts the stated rules. For example, you may tell your students in no uncertain terms that they are not to play with the special materials you will distribute to them until *after* you've given them directions for the project. However, if you pass out the materials—whether it's paint, M&M's, microscopes, or tape recorders—*before* you give instructions, you've invited misbehavior by prolonging the amount of time students have to refrain from using these seductive materials. The procedure you've used to organize the lesson undercuts the behavior you want from the students, and when Clarisse, Eddy, and Frank fool with the microscopes you have to halt instruction to discipline them. However, if you had anticipated the problem and distributed the materials *after* you had given instructions for the project, you would have helped everyone to focus on the instructions and not the materials. Using the concept of "classroom management" helps you to shift your focus from incidents of misbehavior to an examination of everything that occurs in the classroom to support rather than undercut the behavior you want to elicit.

As you're thinking through the rules that you believe must direct the classroom community, you first need to critically examine your expectations. Is the behavior you demand truly essential for your students? Why? Is the conduct you're insisting upon a cultural norm you've simply imported from your own education, or is it a crucial skill the children you work with need to succeed academically? I sometimes see teachers expending considerable energy on enforcing ritual behavior, like having their students rise to say "Good morning" in unison to visitors; but when I've asked the students why they should do this, the children can't explain why they're doing it or why the teachers consider this essential behavior. On the other hand, I worked with a teacher who insisted on this conduct, as part of her emphasis on learning social etiquette, which she defined as treating other people with respect and consideration. In her classroom the ritual was educationally meaningful, an aspect of having "good manners." When students interrupted one another or hurled insults, the teacher identified this behavior as "poor manners" and reminded students of the conduct she expected.

Once you clarify your expectations, you should make sure that your students understand the purpose of this new behavior, which may contradict what they've been told at home or learned from experience. If you defend a prohibition against fighting by telling your students "Fighting is wrong," but they know they must defend themselves with their fists if they're attacked in the park, you're undermining your own legitimacy. In order to succeed in school, students whose culture contrasts sharply with white, middle-class norms of schooling must learn to live in two cultures that require different ways of talking and acting. You can help them by clarifying the differences and similarities, rather than insisting that the school's norms are always the right ones. So instead of saying "Fighting is wrong," and thereby implying that putting up a struggle when someone tries to steal their bike is wrong, you can state that "Fighting isn't allowed in the classroom," explaining why. Even young children can engage in fruitful analysis of standards for judging when fighting is prudent, necessary, and ethical; as a bonus, this discussion will teach you much about their world and values, data you'll find helpful in refining—or perhaps modifying—your case for the behavior you insist upon in your classroom.

You may have to teach your students social skills that you take for granted and that you assume they know, for instance, discussing a dispute rather than insulting someone's appearance. Excellent urban teachers use a wide range of teaching strategies to help their students learn and practice appropriate social interaction, and to make your classroom a well-functioning community you'll have to become adept at using these techniques. One method I've seen teachers at all levels use successfully is having class members role-play an appropriate response to a typical scenario that evokes strong reactions, so that students can experience acting differently in an imagined situation before they are expected to carry out the behavior in real life.

If you're reading this book as part of a college course to prepare you to teach, you may have heard already that well-planned lessons are the heart of effective classroom management. That's even truer in urban schools because many students experience situations at home that make concentrating on academic achievement problematic. Some children have home lives that are unsafe or insecure, emotionally and physically. For other students, especially adolescents, the financial rewards that we assume accompany academic achievement seem (and, in fact, may be) unobtainable: What's the use of graduating from high school if you know dozens of young people who can't find a decent-paying job even with a diploma? Who live in neighborhoods in which drug dealing is the most common means of support?

Another source of distraction from learning is the policy of "ability grouping," or tracking, which reinforces students' lack of confidence in themselves as learners. Although most American schools divide students according to their ostensible ability, the policy is most fully developed in large urban districts, which often extend the practice to include entrance tests for admission to high schools and junior high schools. Children learn the significance of their labels very quickly; the "bluebirds" and the "robins" know what their designations mean in hierarchical terms, who's "smart" and "dumb," and they often perform accordingly.

Before teaching in the New York City schools I wasn't convinced that adolescents' self-image was influenced by tracking. However, I learned differently when I spoke to my students. My students at King, a neighborhood school required to take all students in the zone, chafed at the presence of the High School of Music and Art in a building across the street. They viewed the students at this school, which had a competitive entrance exam, as privileged; fights between students in the schools were a common occurrence. A few years later when I asked a class of students at Humanities High School—like King, a school without selective admissions—why they had chosen the school, one girl called out, "Everyone's here because we didn't get into Stuyvesant or [Bronx High School of] Science or [High School of] Music and Art. No one would make Humanities a *first* choice."

We know from much research that the lower tracks contain a disproportionate number of students who are "involuntary minorities," who are rarely exposed to instruction that calls for high-level cognition, creativity, or choice. These students, whose expectations for themselves mirror the school's minimal expectations, often feel too defeated to even attempt school work. When they are in low tracks in schools that are racially segregated, their feeling of being rejected is almost overwhelming, and they often express their feelings of self-defeat and hopelessness with amazing candor. It's not unusual to hear kids in the lowest tracks make comments like "We don't do much work 'cause we're in the dumb class."

Dealing with School Violence

Beyond excellent classroom management skills that help you keep violent disputes from developing, the key to dealing with violent behavior in the classroom is to know your students and respect them. Consider this: In the years that I taught in New York City I worked with about 2,000 teenagers, many of them from violent neighborhoods, yet I dealt with only one I felt was dangerous. Most of the times when I heard about an incident in which a student physically assaulted a teacher, I knew from my own dealings with the teacher that she or he treated students inhumanely, abusing the teacher's authority—for instance, by reading test scores aloud to embarrass students who had failed or ridiculing them. Here again let me draw a distinction between justifying behavior and explaining it. The behavior of students who assault or threaten teachers (or classmates) can't be justified or tolerated. But what's often overlooked in these situations is that the behavior could have been short-circuited had the teacher been more thoughtful.

If you treat your students with empathy, consideration, and respect, you need not fear them. With most students, violent behavior is a response to a perceived provocation, not a random act, so if you avert confrontations, you avoid violence. Many poor city kids live with a degree of stress and pressure that gives them hair-trigger tempers, and teachers have to keep this is mind when addressing misbehavior. Obviously you don't pursue a disagreement with someone who seems to be on the brink of exploding, even if you are angry yourself. As the adult with authority, you have to step away from the confrontation so that it doesn't escalate. I'd often tell an angry student "We can talk about that after class, in private," so that I retained my authority in front of the class but avoided further conflict. Often the privacy did indeed permit us to negotiate a mutually acceptable settlement.

The most frightening news reports often describe students who bring weapons to school. The experiences I've had with students who've brought weapons into school illustrate that even this kind of behavior, which seems completely inexplicable, doesn't necessarily demonstrate that a student is a thug. I learned this in my first year of teaching in New York City when Danny, a student in my first-period class, was suspended for carrying a knife in school. I was frightened thinking of how Danny, who attended class irregularly, might have used the knife on me or a classmate. As I eavesdropped on a conversation between two colleagues, one of whom had worked with the student in previous years, I heard the situation cast differently. Danny, who was large for his 15 years, took the subway to his full-time job in a distant, dangerous section of the Bronx every day after school. He worked from 3:00 PM to 11:00 PM, six days a week, to support his siblings and infirm mother. Because he had to be at work promptly at 3:00 PM for the shift change, on school days he had no time to go home to pick up the knife, which he needed for protection coming home late at night. A teacher had spotted the knife when it fell out of Danny's pocket, as he bent over in the hallway to pick up a dropped book, and notified a security guard. Danny was suspended automatically, in accordance with a new Board of Education policy passed in response to publicity about unsafe schools.

After his suspension, Danny returned to class for a few sessions. I took the occasion to ask why he was usually absent. He explained he had to help his younger siblings get ready for school, and he was often too tired to awake an hour earlier so that he'd have time to shower and eat himself in time for first period. Until that point, I had never known anyone who regularly carried a weapon, and I realized that I didn't know what I would have done in Danny's situation, especially since the school offered him no help in shouldering the burden of supporting his family while simultaneously trying to finish high school. Although the prohibition against carrying weapons into school was certainly justified, the school never addressed the reasons students violated the regulation. Had the school environment been less anonymous and inflexible and had counselors been available, Danny could have received help that would have helped him avert the suspension. For instance, he might have been given a reduced class schedule, to allow him to come later and leave earlier from school. Another possibility would have been to try to find him a job closer to school and his home, to pare down time lost in his commute.

The incident with Danny proved to be a dress rehearsal for a situation I confronted later that same year, when Sonya, an outspoken, hot-tempered young woman in one of my classes, emptied her purse on a table while searching for an elusive pen. A penknife tumbled out, along with various lipsticks, nail polish, and key chains. Sonya immediately noticed that I had seen the knife and apologized profusely for her indiscretion. When I told her that she shouldn't have the knife in school, she admonished me, saying something like, "You think I'm crazy, to go in the elevator in my building without something to protect me? *You* be there in that dark elevator and hallway with nobody around. You think I'm going to let some joker rape or murder me without no fight?"

I told Sonya that she couldn't have the knife in school without risking suspension and told her to put it away and never let me see it again. I could understand how another teacher might have felt obligated to report the incident, and I worried that if Sonya felt physically threatened in school she might use the knife; but I also knew that Sonya faced a dilemma that the school had ignored. If an adult in the school could sit down with Sonya and try to work out other options, if counselors in the school had connections with security officials in the projects, then reporting her would make a difference because she'd get assistance. In the absence of this support, all that I'd accomplish by enforcing the regulation would be to further alienate Sonya from school and teachers. If she had been suspended and then returned to school, she would certainly have continued to carry the knife because nothing else would have changed. I did not report the incident; instead, I tried to figure out a way to help her get home safely without bringing a knife to school—and crossed my fingers that she would never use the knife in school.

Another incident occurred when I was teaching at King, a few years after these incidents in Richman High School. I saw a student I knew only by sight display a gun to others who had gathered in the hallway outside my room between classes. He observed my glance and quickly hid the gun in his jacket pocket. I raced to call security using the closest phone, in the departmental office, which had been locked as usual by the chairperson, Mr. X; unable to call, I asked a colleague passing by to contact security with the message that I had seen a student carrying a gun. Eventually the gun, which was not loaded, was found in a locker and confiscated; the student was suspended. However, the incident greatly alarmed me, and for days I worried that the student would retaliate against me for reporting him.

In both situations students violated a regulation I fully supported, yet I responded differently. The nature of the violations differed in that Sonya had a penknife and the other student a gun, but on reflection, I think that my reaction was also due to the context of confronting violence. I had a relationship with Sonya and therefore I wasn't frightened by her, though her behavior disturbed me. In the other predicament, I was terrified because the student was a stranger to me. I think these incidents illustrate that as soon as your students become people to you, your decisions about punishment and discipline change; but you can deal with your students as human beings and individuals only if you are not afraid of them, and racial and class differences frequently make us fear people with whom we have no personal relations.

One of the reasons I strongly advise that prospective urban teachers become comfortable with the kinds of students they're going to be teaching before they assume a position of authority, even as a student teacher, is that when we can see our students as human beings like ourselves rather than as "the other," we can separate the person from the act and intervene appropriately. When I spotted Sonya's knife I was scared because I'm not accustomed to being with people who carry weapons and know that their presence dramatically escalates the risks of bodily harm in arguments. However, I wasn't afraid of Sonya, and therefore I could analyze, rationally, how best to handle the situation. On the other hand, when I saw the student displaying a gun in the hallway, I feared him and the behavior, because I didn't know him personally. In retrospect, I think my qualms about retribution were inflated by the social gulf between us.

I've only once been able to explore this topic with a group of experienced urban teachers in a racially and socially mixed class. In one course I taught at Jersey City State College, my students and I had some wonderfully candid, thoughtful discussions about how race affects our interactions with students. In one particularly frank session following our reading of John Ogbu's work, I related an experience to help us think through the implications of racial differences between teachers and students. When I returned to King High School as a visitor after teaching college for several years, I found myself frightened at the sea of noisy, black teenagers flooding out of the building at the end of the day. As I grappled with my anxiety, I recalled that I had felt the same way on the first few weeks teaching there. The feeling wore off without my noticing it was gone, and I had forgotten it entirely until it returned after my long absence. I remembered that when I taught at King some of my white friends had expressed their apprehension at being around crowds of black teenagers and had wondered aloud to me why I wasn't afraid.

The African American teachers in my college class, mothers and fathers of teenagers, made comments that showed that they were either bemused or a bit offended that anyone would find a crowd of black teenagers frightening. The white teachers, most of whom taught in schools in which white students were a minority, did not enter into the conversation, so I don't know what they were thinking. I struggled to answer the question of what had frightened me, what would scare middle-aged white people, about being with black teenagers when Mildred, a middle-aged black woman raised in a small town in the South, related an anecdote that revealed a similar response—to white teenagers. Mildred was driving her daughter home from college late at night and decided to save time by exiting from the highway on an unfamiliar road that took her through a nearby white working-class community. On this warm June night she saw a large cluster of young white males, sitting on their cars and the sidewalks, drinking beer and shouting to one another. She was panic-stricken, fearing for her daughter and her safety as she stopped for a red light; she zoomed off at a high speed as soon as the light changed. Mildred and I agreed that if I had been in her situation and she in mine, neither of us would have been frightened.

For both of us, the feeling of racial isolation provoked a deep fear. I think for many young, white, middle-class teachers, the same occurs when they begin their careers in racially segregated schools. They fear their students but are ashamed to admit it, even if they can find someone to talk with, which they can't. Our society is supposed to be based on ideals of racial and social equality, and acknowledging that our behavior contradicts those ideals can be humiliating. We live in a society that is racially segregated, and few people have friends of different races with whom we talk about race frankly. To make matters worse, the culture in most schools makes pointed discussion of race almost a taboo, especially when the teaching staff is predominantly white and the students African American. As some interesting research indicates, even when teachers are explicitly committed to working through racial divisions, to creating "safe spaces" to analyze attitudes about race, the lack of models about how to operate is a daunting challenge.

When teachers are intimidated by their students, they're unable to address problem behavior straightforwardly because their fear is paralyzing. In my experience working with new teachers who are afraid of their students but unwilling to admit it, the strategy most adopt is to ignore the misconduct. But all of a teacher's words and actions are educative, and when teachers consistently disregard students' inappropriate behavior, they're actually sending a message to the unruly student that the conduct will be accepted. Children know when teachers fear them and resent it because the fear is demeaning in its reversal of appropriate adult–child relations. The misbehaving child is not receiving suitable guidance from the adult in authority, and he or she realizes it, perhaps more quickly than the adult.

Establishing Your Moral Authority

The options a teacher has to punish misconduct are quite limited, though probably not much more so than they were a hundred years ago. After all, the most draconian punishments, like striking children or expelling them, can't be exercised often, even when they're legal. Though historians have demonstrated that the problem of disruptive students isn't a new phenomenon, I think the problem of establishing control in the classroom is a greater challenge today.

One enormous change is that for the first time in our history as a nation, American society is legally committed to providing *all* children with equal educational opportunities. Before the civil rights movement succeeded in eliminating legally sanctioned segregation, before bilingual and special education became legal requirements, if students were viewed as troublesome, they were excluded from schools. In addition, most white Americans didn't need much formal schooling because decent-paying jobs didn't require academic credentials. Teachers today have to know how to teach types of kids that American society has never before attempted to educate, yet the school structure has not changed to accommodate this challenge.

I often hear new teachers, especially those who have attended paro-chial schools with classmates who shared a similar cultural background, angrily recall that "When I was growing up, I did what the teacher said, or *else*!" They are stunned and frustrated that as teachers their decisions aren't automatically obeyed. What they have to consider is that as public school teachers they have an obligation to work with *all* students, includ-ing the sort who were expelled from the private schools they attended. Another factor is that parochial schools have an explicit moral vision that parents must endorse and that the school promotes. The teacher is given her authority by the institution, which parents trust and support.

Years ago, teachers could rely more on the power of their position, or what is called their "uniformed authority," to impose their will in the classroom. Their role as teacher gave them a significant degree of control, just as the police officer's uniform (even without the holster) confers power. Students who are voluntary minorities from countries in which only a tiny proportion of the population is educated beyond basic literacy and numeracy often display a respect for the teacher's "uniformed" au-thority: Regardless of how well teachers perform, they are highly re-spected, even revered; the teacher's word is never disputed. However, when the teacher's "uniformed" authority is rejected or challenged, as it is among students and families who are mistrustful of schools, the teacher has to rely on two other sources of control: "moral" and "technical" authority.

People exert "technical" authority when their clients believe them to be far more expert about the service being rendered. We don't generally question the doctor's diagnosis because we acknowledge that the doctor has access to knowledge and skills that we don't. As with "uniformed" authority, "technical" authority is of relatively little value to urban teach-ers, in part because so many issues in curriculum and instruction are disputed. For instance, even if you are well acquainted with the vast literature on teaching reading, you can't defend a decision to use a certain approach purely on the basis of scholarship because another school district 20 miles away may well be using a system that's based on a contradictory set of assumptions. Another limitation to technical authority is that stu-dents who are already alienated from school are not likely to be convinced to do as the teacher says because of his or her superior knowledge of the subject area or teaching.

Urban teachers' primary source of control is their "moral" authority, which rests on the perception of students and parents that the teacher is knowledgeable about the subject matter, competent in pedagogy, and committed to helping all students succeed, in school and life. As I've stressed throughout this book, teachers' actions can be interpreted differently by different kinds of students, so although a teacher's deeds may be proof positive to him or her of dedicated performance, students and parents may have a contradictory perception. I learned this the hard way when I unknowingly offended an African American student in one of my classes at Humanities High School with a jocular reprimand I made to a classmate. The remark was a stock comment I had used many times at King, to my students' great pleasure, and I was stunned and hurt that my remark could be taken as racist. After some painful reflection, I realized that my remark was indeed thoughtless and that certain teaching behaviors that had served me well at King would be perceived differently by the more middle-class student population at Humanities.

What you think is caring behavior may not be perceived as such by your students and parents. Racial, gender, and class differences between teachers and students, power inequities in their relationship to one another, and the school's insularity all converge to make communication difficult, so disparate perceptions of actions are common. Establishing your moral authority depends on your ability to view your own performance from your students' and parents' eyes. Remember Mrs. M, who carried armloads of practice exams home to correct? That's a perfect example of an action that to some teachers is clear evidence of dedication; but to many of her students Mrs. M was simply forcing them to do yet another tedious exercise, exercising her power as the teacher. Her reminders about the importance of the exam were taken as scolding. Yet the same notification from another teacher was understood as an indication of concern.

As my experience at Humanities illustrates, there's no formula for insuring that your performance will be perceived as you intend it; however, the more conscious you are of the problem of isolation, of the ways suspicions are fed by disparities in gender, race, and class, the more capable you'll be of establishing classroom routines and methods of dealing with your students that convey your dedication and win their trust. Your moral authority is based on your ability to demonstrate to your students and their parents that in your role as teacher you intend to assist each of your students—and that you are capable of doing so. When you make instruction engaging and worthwhile and when you establish a classroom environment that is based on mutual respect, you establish your moral authority, which gives you more control and authority than the threat or use of punishment.

This may seem hopelessly idealistic or Pollyanna-ish to some readers, so I hope two examples from my experience will persuade you differently. Unlike most high school teachers, I've always enjoyed decorating my classroom and keeping art supplies on hand for special projects. I noticed that few city teachers kept anything more than a pencil in their desks, even when they didn't travel between classrooms and had a room of their own. When I asked a few I was told that nothing was safe unless it was locked up, including pens and pencils. One or two people told me not to decorate my room because posters would be vandalized or stolen. I decided that I couldn't work in an environment of such mistrust, but on the other hand, I knew that leaving expensive equipment, like my small tape recorder, in an unlocked place was an invitation to theft.

I decided to act as I had throughout my previous years of teaching. I locked up in a closet all the items that would be tempting targets, like my purse and electronic equipment and the class set of pocket dictionaries I had bought with my own money. Everything else, including my valued art pencils and desk supplies, stayed in my desk. In addition, I usually kept a few dollars in change in an envelope in the top drawer, to buy raffles or make donations when students were collecting for a worthwhile cause. As I had in the suburbs, I decorated my classroom walls with art and movie posters I knew the students would like, as well as displays of their work. The only difference in my behavior was that on the first day of class, when I introduced myself to the students, I asked them to look around the room and tell me what they saw. Students remarked that they disliked the boring (their word) sterility (my word) of most classrooms and enjoyed working in a room that looked more like a home. I responded that I had spent my money and time decorating the room so that we could all enjoy being in a room that made us feel better about ourselves, and just as when we invite someone into our home we expect respect and consideration for our belongings, I expected that they would treat my decorations and property respectfully. To be certain that they understood my expectations, I described the behavior I wanted: No one would go into my desk without asking; no one would write on or deface anything on the walls; anyone who borrowed materials would return them in the same condition they were in when taken. In return I would continue to make sure the room was a pleasant working environment for us.

In my 7 subsequent years of city teaching, only once was anything taken from my desk (the money, when I was on jury duty) or a decoration vandalized during class. Although I sat at my desk infrequently during class, I didn't worry that students would steal supplies from it, and they didn't. My trust in them was rewarded, as yours will be if you exercise your authority with concern for their self-respect, dignity, and sense of earned accomplishment, with attention to the human needs and desires we all share.

8 Your Moral and Political Obligations

After reading my descriptions of the problems you'll face as an urban teacher, you may be rethinking your decision to teach in an urban school. I can hear some of my friends who are career teachers say "Everything you've said is accurate; but Lo, if you tell them all this, anyone who's sane won't want to teach in the city!" They have a point, and I'm reminded of what occurred during the Italian campaign in World War II when the Army commissioned a well-known filmmaker to create a documentary that would show soldiers what battle would be like: After showing it a few times, the Army suppressed the film because it terrified the soldiers it was supposed to inform.

Unlike soldiers who are drafted during war, city teachers enlist voluntarily, and I hope people won't take on the job if they haven't thought seriously about the demands that will be made on them and wrestled with their conscience about the extent to which they are willing to extend themselves to children they must serve. Every so often in my college classes I come across new and prospective teachers whose stance toward teaching is that it's a job that's not so different from any other civil service position. They make light of the moral tensions inherent in urban teaching and have decided in advance that their responsibilities are clear-cut and there's no dilemma created for teachers when the effectiveness of education is predicated on their self-sacrifice. Frankly, I don't want people to become city teachers if they don't see that almost every day of their career they'll be called on to make decisions about how much they can and should do to help their students. Although I've described the many ways in which teaching is a job and teachers are treated as workers, it also has moral dimensions we associate with careers that are referred to as "callings."

It may seem like the job of teaching as I've described it is more than a person should be asked to handle for a lifetime, and indeed, it may be. I know of only a handful of city teachers who have made a lifetime career of teaching and thrived in the classroom until they retired. Many more who remain in the classroom have ceased taking much pleasure from their work. I think that in the majority of city schools serving the highest proportions of children from impoverished, violent neighborhoods, the conditions are so wearing that it's utopian to expect teachers to sustain their dedication and idealism for 30 years. Just a handful of children in these schools overcome the staggeringly great social, economic, and educational barriers that impede academic achievement, and a similarly small number of dedicated teachers start and end their teaching careers with the same degree of enthusiasm and commitment with which they began in these schools.

I suggest that you don't assume that you'll be doing the same job in 3 decades. You may enjoy teaching in a city school enormously after you become proficient, but after several years you may weary of the routine, as well as the disparity between what you're expected to do and the support that you're provided. It's unfair and educationally indefensible that city teachers are treated like disposable commodities, but they are, and at the start of this challenge you're assuming, you should be clear-eyed about what you've undertaken. When teaching no longer provides you with a strong sense of satisfaction, when you feel worn out by the responsibility, it's time for you to intervene. The school system itself doesn't help teachers to renew themselves, so they must monitor and take charge of their professional and psychological well-being independently. To revitalize themselves, some teachers return to school as full-time students for another degree, in a field related to teaching or another area they're considering as an alternative occupation. One friend takes unpaid leaves to travel the world whenever she can afford it. Another colleague took off a year to work in personnel and found that although she could easily earn more money in this occupation, she missed being in school; her year away helped her identify satisfactions about the job she hadn't previously noticed. Another strategy is to make a lateral move into another school-based occupation, such as counseling. Other teachers, like myself, leave K–12 teaching for the college level or careers in the private sector.

People who remain in the classroom when they no longer want to be there are among the most unhappy workers you'll ever meet. Teaching has quite modest rewards outside of the satisfaction of feeling that you've connected with your students; and when this pleasure diminishes for urban teachers, the negative aspects of the job become overwhelming. Two months off in the summer, job security, and a decent pension can't compensate for 10 months of feeling hostile toward and unappreciated by your students, though some people try to convince themselves that this is the case. When you start to identify the students as the source of your frustration, and the pleasures you receive from your teaching don't compensate for the frustrations, change your career.

Some educational researchers and teacher educators write about the need for teachers to be "change agents" who take leadership in improving conditions in the school. I take issue with this perspective because I know that learning to teach in an urban school is a job-and-a-half. Especially in the first years of urban teaching, new teachers have little time or energy for anything beyond survival. Another problem with this "change agent" strategy for reforming schools is that it focuses on the role of teachers as individuals, but urban teachers face a formidable bureaucracy, and more than one fine teacher has found that battling the school bureaucracy is a Promethean struggle.

Many of the best teachers feel that they satisfy their moral and professional obligations by serving their students well. They focus completely and wholeheartedly on their students' well-being and their teaching. Their professional lives, and sometimes their personal lives, too, are dominated by their direct involvement with the children they teach or their classroom responsibilities. These teachers render invaluable service to the schools and their students; without their dedication, urban schools would be far worse. Still, I encourage you to adopt an orientation toward school reform that moves beyond this singular focus on your own classroom or students.

The conditions in urban schools that sabotage effective, engaging teaching and learning won't be improved unless teachers and their organizations take leadership for redirecting public debate and policy making. There's not room here for me to enumerate the ways in which current debate and policy are skewed, but I must briefly touch on two areas, inclusion and education of second-language learners. In both of these groups, educational opportunities have been extended to children who were until fairly recently shunted aside by schools. They have won a place in the public schools because parents and advocacy groups agitated for them to be included in the nation's definition of equal opportunity. These children have always been present, but they and their needs were ignored until legislation was passed to extend the right of a free public education to them.

Unfortunately, educational regulations intended to help these students are often conceptually flawed or poorly implemented. Programs to serve handicapped and second-language learners have been glued onto dysfunctional school systems. A colleague once described dealing with the New York City Board of Education as being like wrestling with an octopus that has no head: It's not possible to escape the tentacles and it's also not possible to get at a nerve center. New programs that are added become additional tentacles, creating enormous new problems for already over-extended classroom teachers.

When I have asked teachers in my college courses to choose an important school problem for a research project, more than half select teaching second-language learners and inclusion of special education students.

What they discover in their research is that when the programs are implemented so that teachers receive adequate training, when they provide appropriate financial support, when they encourage collaboration among teachers, parents, and students, so that educational decisions are made on an individual basis, the programs improve education—for everyone. However, more often than not city teachers are presented with poorly planned programs as a *fait accompli*. They have students with severe disabilities added to their already overcrowded classrooms; no provisions are made for support, for either the students or teacher. They see their students who do not speak or write English well pulled from their classroom for tutoring that is wholly separate from ongoing work in the classroom, often by a teacher who is not proficient in English.

Complaints such as these can be used by some teachers as excuses for jettisoning our responsibilities to serve all students well, but the most caring and competent teachers also observe that the programs that are supposed to be helping children who have particular needs are failing them. I've experienced the frustration of having students who speak no English in my classroom, and I know how much more difficult teaching is when the classroom serves students with significant physical handicaps. Martin Luther King, Jr., High School was housed in a modern building that had elevators and was wheelchair accessible, so we were one of the few Manhattan high schools that students in wheelchairs could attend. Both times that my classes contained a student in a wheelchair, I spent twice as much effort in teaching the class because of complications no one assisted me in handling. For instance, I made a point of stressing punctuality and began class when the bell rang. Because the halls were frequently noisy with students who were late to their classes calling out to friends in my class, I'd often have to lock the door shortly after the bell rang. Due to problems with the elevator or the bus that transported them, students in wheelchairs were often absent. When they did come to class, they often arrived 10 or 15 minutes after the period began. Their entry invariably created a disturbance because while the door was being held open, a student passing through the hall would beckon or insult someone in my class.

I had to struggle not to resent the students in wheelchairs because of the additional work their presence caused me. Yet it would be hard to find someone more sympathetic than I to inclusion because of my personal knowledge of what life was like for handicapped children before passage of legislation guaranteeing their educational opportunities. My younger sister is blind, and I recall clearly the sacrifices families had to make to educate their handicapped children. Children who were mentally retarded were frequently hidden at home and not educated at all; kids with physical handicaps had to attend boarding schools at a young age. One of my sister's friends attended my junior high and high school, and her mother went with her, to escort her from class to class and to take notes that she later Brailled. The family was responsible for obtaining, when they could, copies of books in Braille from the Library of Congress. The school had no responsibility to help—and didn't. Few of the dozen or so blind children my sister's age received more than a grade school education. Today most spend their days at home; a few work in sheltered workshops. Of the entire cohort, two or three live independently and work in regular jobs.

I know first-hand how critically important the legislation expanding the nation's commitment to educational opportunity has been for tens of thousands of children. Yet I can empathize with the resentment teachers feel and can see how they often conclude, erroneously, that the solution is to eliminate special programs, to keep special education students isolated, to force non-native speakers to sink or swim in English. When my students realize that the programs could be conceptualized and operated differently—as indeed they are in wealthy, suburban school systems—they express great frustration. They agree that students who aren't native speakers of English and those who are handicapped should receive a quality education, but they also see no way for that to occur unless urban schooling is totally transformed.

Unfortunately, in many instances the unions that represent teachers have adopted a hostile stance toward the demand for expanding educational opportunities to groups that have not been adequately served by urban schools. Although the unions state that they want to make educational equality a reality, they've done little or nothing to protect students who've been victimized by the status quo. The teacher unions have tended to be active on issues of equity only *after* legislation has been passed, when they (correctly) point out the abuses and problems. By failing to employ their political resources to defend the rights of handicapped children and students excluded from schools because they didn't speak English, the unions forfeited the opportunity to shape policy, to make sure that the laws and programs would be effective.

The dynamic I've described has characterized the relationship between urban teacher unions and progressive social change for the past 30 years. Rather than seeing itself as an ally and participant in the struggle of activists who are trying to make urban schools serve all children well, the teachers union more often than not either remains neutral, adopts a tepid paper position in support, or opposes the change. As a result, teacher unions have a poor reputation among many advocates of progressive school reform and have little legitimacy in the public's eye.

Teachers have access to insider knowledge of schools that parents and citizens don't, and their perspective and participation are essential for reforms that truly improve schools. Our unions and professional organizations have to be proactive in working with groups who defend the interests of children because unless we work together, little will change to help city teachers and their students succeed. The teachers unions in most cities are lethargic and bereft of educational vision, in part because they've accommodated to the narrow role spelled out in the laws that give teachers the right to form unions and bargain collectively. It's difficult to imagine that these tired organizations could be revitalized, and perhaps they can't with the existing leadership. But as long as the organizations that are supposed to represent urban teachers fail to support the rights of the neediest kids, teachers will face the dilemma of defending existing conditions at the expense of students who've been excluded from the promise of educational opportunity.

When teachers unions began to organize city teachers in the 1960s, they used the slogan "Teachers want what children need." When the union allies itself with groups struggling to include all children in America's educational promises, I think it demonstrates the slogan's accuracy. I hope that as you teach you'll think about holding your union to its social and political obligations to city kids.

As I was writing this chapter, I had a casual conversation with the white, middle-class father of two children who attend a Manhattan public school known for its innovative curriculum and the wealth of the neighborhood it serves. He commented glowingly that the principal requires all teachers in his children's school to stay until 6:00 P.M. every day. When I suggested that this couldn't be the case, he altered his statement: The principal only hires those teachers who are willing to stay until 6:00 P.M. Earlier in our conversation he had informed me that his wife teaches special education in a Brooklyn school that I know is attended by working-class and poor children. As he approvingly reported on the excellence of his children's education, I silently wondered if his wife stayed until 6:00 P.M. in her school. I wouldn't tell him or his wife that she *should* remain long past the end of the school day, because city teachers should not be forced to sacrifice a full personal life for their teaching. However, I was struck by the paradox and the utter lack of thoughtfulness in his boast.

As parents and citizens, we expect schools to serve our children well, but under present conditions providing children with a quality education means that teachers must make considerable sacrifices. Because of their knowledge of school life and their position within the school system, teachers are irreplaceable in the struggles that must occur to eliminate the conditions that deter them from serving kids well. As an urban teacher, shouldn't you be part of this effort to transform urban schools?

About the Author

Lois Weiner teaches education at New Jersey City University, where she coordinates the program preparing secondary teachers for urban schools. She completed her undergraduate work at the University of California, Berkeley, and the University of Stockholm, Sweden, and her teaching preparation at California State University, Hayward. She received her M.A. at Teachers College, Columbia University, and her Ed.D. from Harvard University. During the fifteen years in which she taught high school English in California, in New York City, and in two suburbs of New York, she was an active member of the teachers union. She lives in Manhattan and enjoys cooking and swimming year-round, and reading nineteenth-century novels in the summer. Currently she is revising her earlier book, *Preparing Teachers for Urban Schools* (Teachers College Press, 1993).